PROPHETIC INSIGHTS FOR DAILY LIVING

VOLUME 5

~~

Inspired Messages From The Holy Spirit

Sheila Eismann

Books by Sheila Eismann

A STORMY YEAR – BOOK 2 OF THE SABBLONTI SERIES

A WOMAN OF SUBSTANCE – A 12-WEEK BIBLE STUDY

CREATIVE AUTHORS' WORKBOOK JOURNAL – A STEP-BY-STEP GUIDE FOR YOUR WRITING EXPERIENCE – CO-AUTHOR

HEART TO HEART FROM GOD'S WORD

LOVE, THE TIE THAT BINDS – BOOK 3 OF THE SABBLONTI SERIES

JANTZI'S JOKERS – BOOK 1 OF THE SABBLONTI SERIES

POETRY TIME – VOLUME ONE

PROPHETIC INSIGHTS FOR DAILY LIVING – MESSAGES INSPIRED BY THE HOLY SPIRIT – VOLUME 1

PROPHETIC INSIGHTS FOR DAILY LIVING – MESSAGES INSPIRED BY THE HOLY SPIRIT – VOLUME 2

PROPHETIC INSIGHTS FOR DAILY LIVING – MESSAGES INSPIRED BY THE HOLY SPIRIT – VOLUME 3

PROPHETIC INSIGHTS FOR DAILY LIVING – MESSAGES INSPIRED BY THE HOLY SPIRIT – VOLUME 4

PROPHETIC INSIGHTS FOR DAILY LIVING – MESSAGES INSPIRED BY THE HOLY SPIRIT – VOLUME 5

RECOGNIZE YOUR CIRCLES

STIRRINGS OF THE SPIRIT

Sheila Eismann

STRAIGHT FROM THE HORSE'S TROUGH

THE CHRISTMAS TIN

Copyright © 2022 by Sheila Eismann.

www.sheilaeismann.com

All rights reserved. No portion of this book may be reproduced, stored in a retrieval system, or transmitted in any form or by any means — electronic, mechanical, photocopy, recording, scanning, or other — except for brief quotations in critical reviews or articles, without the prior written permission of the publisher.

Published by Desert Sage Press
www.desertsagepress.com

Printed and bound in the United States of America.

Cover design by Cathie Richardson. www.countrygardenstitchery.com
All rights reserved.

Any trademarks, service marks, product names, or named features are used only for reference, and are assumed to be the property of their respective owners, and the use of any one of those terms does not imply an endorsement on the part of the author and/or the publisher.

ISBN: 978-1-7373135-4-0

Library of Congress Control Number: 2022915863

Scriptures are taken from the New King James Version. Copyright 1979, 1980, 1982 by Thomas Nelson, Inc. Used by permission. All rights reserved.

Scripture quotations marked (NIV) are taken from the Holy Bible, New International Version®, NIV®. Copyright © 1973, 1978, 1984, 2011 by Biblica, Inc.® Used by permission of Zondervan. All rights reserved worldwide. www.zondervan.com. The "NIV" and "New International Version" are trademarks registered in the United States Patent and Trademark Office by Biblica, Inc.®

DEDICATION

    This series of workbooks is dedicated to my beloved husband, Dan, who our precious grandkiddos affectionately refer to as "Poppy." He's my best friend, confidant, loyal companion, and fellow believer in our Lord and Savior, Jesus Christ. I will be forever grateful for God knitting our hearts together in His love and giving us compatible and mutually beneficial spiritual giftings.
    We've experienced challenges, supreme blessings, miracles, and victories during the 39 years of our marriage. God has sustained us every single day and step of the way by His mighty right hand, His beloved Son, Jesus Christ, The Holy Spirit, His Word, and His ministering angels.
    We're eternally grateful for all of the divine appointments God has orchestrated with those of His choosing throughout the intersections of our lives.
    It's been the honor and privilege of a lifetime to walk side-by-side with Dan as we continue to learn, laugh, and love together. To God be the glory, both now and forevermore!

ACKNOWLEDGEMENTS

My heartfelt gratitude, sincere appreciation, and blessings are extended to Cathie Richardson, Lesta Chadez, and Marilyn Battisti for their invaluable assistance and encouragement in publishing this set of prophetic workbooks.

It's been a special joy to share this experience with my oldest daughter, Cathie, whose artistic gifts and talents bless me beyond measure. For a real treat, please check out her website: **www.countrygardenstitchery.com**

Fifty-three years ago, Lesta and I lived in the same small rural area. Our paths reconnected at just the right time. Despite navigating her own set of life's challenges, Lesta's dynamic combination of mercy and exhortation is a bonus for any writer. In addition, she's a poet, author, and spiritual songwriter.

Being a retired school teacher, Marilyn operates from a unique vantage point with respect to almost everything she reads and studies, especially as it relates to spiritual matters. I continue to be amazed when reading her thoughts if she opts to post a comment on my website after I've authored one of my blog posts! Since Marilyn has a real heart for intercessory prayer, she's blessed my life immensely as a prayer partner.

In addition, I want to thank my Lord Jesus for helping me every day in every way. With Him, all things are possible. (Matthew 19:26) I'm grateful for The Holy Spirit and His gifts of creativity which are inherent within each of us in various forms.

TABLE OF CONTENTS

Introduction	13
Prophetic Vision – 5 Standing Dominoes	27
Free The Fish	37
Soak, Seek, & Serve	46
A Key Over Tennessee	56
The Baker & The Five Loaves	65
A Coat of Many Colors	76
Holy Week Gifts	86
An Adjustment To Your Spiritual Wedding Garment	95
T. F. T. ~ Today For Tomorrow	105
Prophetic Dream – Norm, Debbie, & The Dinner	117
Large & In Charge	127
It's Cool To Be Kind!	135
The Way Of Life Winds Upward For The Wise	145
The Angel, The Basket, & The Scrolls	156
Grace On Our Lips	167
Hold The Dream!	176
The Angel With The Pocket Watch	186
Living In A Field Of Faith	196
About The Author	209
Other Books Available from Sheila and Dan Eismann & Desert Sage Press	211

Notes and Reflections 218

FOREWARD

Woven into the fabric of our lives wherein a silver cord is intertwined throughout the tapestry, there are people in our circle of friends where our hearts are bound together through the Holy Spirit. Sheila Eismann is a special friend that God has placed in my life as the Lord has knit our hearts together in His love. We grew up in the same rural town, and our parents were friends. From this friendship, a bond of love was birthed.

As I have read Sheila's books and followed her writings and blogs over the years, her prophetic visions and dreams have ministered to me in many areas. I give praise to our Lord and Savior Jesus Christ for the many ways He has been with me throughout my life. The Lord especially filled my heart with a living hope through a time of testing when my husband entered into his eternal home in 2019. Special friends like Sheila prayed for me through this difficult journey, and I will be forever grateful for the many ways the Lord has strengthened me and given me hope.

Sheila has a gifting and unique way of weaving in words of wisdom, encouragement, and exhortation as she shares with us what the Lord has given her in visions, dreams, and prophetic words. When we face times of trouble, testing, or tribulation, she has a way of bringing her messages to a practical application in our daily lives by sharing words of comfort and hope while challenging us to pursue a deeper walk with the Lord.

The prophetic visions and dreams the Lord has shared with Sheila are for anyone who wants a fresh infusion of faith and strength to start each day. They are for those walking through difficult seasons of life such as loneliness, grief, or change. The wisdom the Lord shares with her may be for those who are overwhelmed by life's challenges and for those who may be concerned about loved ones or the condition of the world around us. When it seems like the circumstances of life and the storms that surround us are pulling us under, she reminds us that the Lord is the Victor and encourages us to continue to put our trust and hope in Him as He is faithful and true to His promises and His Holy Word.

Every day we need wisdom and fresh insight as we walk out the fullness of our salvation in our journey through this earthly life. The workbooks that Sheila has prepared can be as a devotional and also used in a Bible study. Her prophetic writings will be a blessing to those who have open hearts ready to receive what the Lord has for them.

Lesta Chadez, Poet, Spiritual Song Writer, and Author of *Treasures Hidden In Plain Sight, A Collection of Poems and Short Stories*.

You will be ever so blessed to read the prophetic articles by Sheila Eismann. Each of her visions is a timely message to guide and direct you in your everyday living. Having the inspiration from The Holy Spirit, each of Sheila's writings is a direct appointment for you to individually meet with our Lord Jesus and find manna for your soul. Sheila's prophetic visions will definitely inspire you and lift you to another level of Christianity!

Marilyn Battisti, Retired Educator

INTRODUCTION

Prophetic Insights For Daily Living was written with you, the spiritual seeker, Bible reader, and student, in mind to render assistance regarding spiritual gifts, dreams, visions, and prophetic words.

To introduce this new series of workbooks, I deem it's important to go into greater detail concerning the three revelatory gifts of the Holy Spirit listed in 1 Corinthians 12:4-11. These gifts are the word of wisdom, the word of knowledge, and the discerning of spirits.

"There are diversities of gifts, but the same Spirit. There are differences of ministries, but the same Lord. And there are diversities of activities, but it is the same God who works all in all. But the manifestation of the Spirit is given to each one for the profit *of all:* **for to one is given the word of wisdom through the Spirit, to another the word of knowledge through the same Spirit**, to another faith by the same Spirit, to another gifts of healings by the same Spirit, to another the working of miracles, to another prophecy, **to another discerning of spirits**, to another *different* kinds of tongues, to another the interpretation of tongues. But one and the same Spirit works all these things, distributing to each one individually as He wills." [Emphasis mine]

Writing to the church at Corinth, Paul said, "Now concerning spiritual *gifts*, brethren, I do not want you to be ignorant:" [1 Corinthians 12:1]

During its establishment phase, God did not want the church in Corinth to be ignorant concerning these matters, and His desire is no less for present-day churches or Bible-believing Christians.

An important aspect to remember is the Holy Spirit distributes His gifts to each one individually as He wills. [1 Corinthians 12:11] Every single one of the spiritual gifts outlined in 1 Corinthians 12:4-10 is precisely just that, a gift which cannot be bought, traded, manufactured, contrived, manipulated, or you fill in the blank.

<u>The Holy Spirit gift of the word of wisdom and the gift of the word of knowledge:</u>

"Before we begin our study of the gifts of the Holy Spirit, it is important for us to understand that in the scriptures there is a mingling of gifts, so much so that at times we may question just which gift (or gifts) is being manifested. This need cause us no real concern, for it must be remembered that all of the gifts flow from the same source, The Holy Spirit. If we are unable to identify exactly and classify perfectly, let us not be overly concerned. As humans, it is our nature to draw neat lines of separation and classification, but when we seek to impose this practice upon God, we only frustrate ourselves, and we may generate unnecessary confusion.

The word of wisdom and the word of knowledge are two gifts that often work together. Throughout the Old Testament when the prophets would prophesy, the word of wisdom and the word of knowledge would flow together (knowledge, and what to do about it.) In reading the prophetic books of the Old Testament, you will notice the phrase time and time again, "The WORD of the Lord came to _____ (name)." Examples of this can be found in 1 Kings 17:8; Jeremiah 1:4-8; Ezekiel 1:3; Joel 1:1 and Haggai 1:1.

In the New Testament, much of the writings of Paul, Peter, James, and Jude are the word of wisdom and word of knowledge. Also, John's letters to the churches in Revelation chapters 2-3 are this mixture. The word of wisdom often comes with the word of knowledge so that believers in Christ will know how to apply that knowledge correctly. These gifts are two of the three gifts that 'reveal' something. We call these gifts revelation gifts because they consist of information supernaturally revealed from God. Each of these gifts is the God-given ability to receive from Him facts concerning something, anything, about which it is humanly impossible for us to know, revealed to the believer so that he or she may be protected, pray more effectively, or help someone in need.

The gift of the word of knowledge is supernatural in character. It is not obtained by logic, or deduction, reasoning, etc., or by natural senses, but by supernatural revelation through The Holy Spirit. It is the sheer gift of God. It is not essentially a vocal gift. It is received quietly and inaudibly within the person's spirit. It may become vocal when shared with others.

A basic definition of the word of knowledge: a fragment or small item of God's knowledge, supernaturally revealed to a person by The Holy Spirit.

An example of a spoken word of knowledge can be found in John 1:47-49:

'Jesus saw Nathanael coming toward Him, and said of him, 'Behold, an Israelite indeed, in whom is no deceit!'

Nathanael said to Him, 'How do You know me?'

Jesus answered and said to him, 'Before Philip called you, when you were under the fig tree, I saw you.'

Nathanael answered and said to Him, 'Rabbi, You are the Son of God! You are the King of Israel!'

It is important to consider what the word of knowledge is not:

- It is not human knowledge gained by natural means.

- It is not human knowledge sanctified by God.

- It cannot be gained by intellectual learning, studying books, or pursuing academics.

- It is not the ability to study, understand, or interpret the Bible.

- It is not a psychic phenomenon or extra-sensory perception such as telepathy (the supposed ability to be able to read minds), clairvoyance (the supposed ability to know things that are happening elsewhere), or precognition (the supposed ability to know the future.)

The gifts of the Spirit defy human scientific explanation and are not acquired by ordinary educational processes. No amount of education or learning can produce them. They are not dependent upon innate human qualities. For example, the word of wisdom might be spoken by a person or even less than ordinary wisdom. They are not accentuated natural talents and abilities. The least talented or able may as likely be the agent through whom God works as the most intellectually endowed.

It is a subtle ploy of the great deceiver of our souls to attempt to humanize the supernatural and to reduce the spiritual gifts to the level of mere human endowments, talents, and learned or acquired abilities.

A word of knowledge may be revealed to a believer in any of the following ways:

- A sudden inspiration or a deep inner impression.

- A dream, vision, or picture seen through the eye of the spirit, with the interpretation of what is seen.

- Hearing the voice of God, or of angels, audibly or in the ear of the spirit.

- A living personal word from the Lord through scripture.

- The vocal gifts of the Holy Spirit such as tongues, interpretation of tongues, or prophecy. [1 Corinthians 12:10]

Supernatural visions and dreams are usually the word of wisdom or word of knowledge in operation. Acts 2:17-18 reminds us of what was spoken by the prophet Joel,

> *'And it shall come to pass in the last days, says God,*
> *That I will pour out of My Spirit on all flesh;*
> *Your sons and your daughters shall prophesy,*
> *Your young men shall see visions,*
> *Your old men shall dream dreams.*
> *And on My menservants and on My maidservants*
> *I will pour out My Spirit in those days;*
> *And they shall prophesy.'*

The word of knowledge may not always be fully understood by the receiver or the hearers. It can seem like it's a riddle or a mystery. In the seventh and eighth chapters of the book of Daniel, we read where the prophet was troubled in his spirit, and the visions that were given to him disturbed him greatly. In Daniel 8:27b, God's servant was appalled by the vision, and it was beyond his understanding.

Oftentimes God will use a word of knowledge to uncover sin, bring people to Him, give guidance and direction, minister encouragement, or impart knowledge of future events. Some Bible scholars teach the revelation of future events to be the gift of the word of wisdom rather than the word of knowledge since wisdom usually pertains to what to do in the future.

If you would like to take the time to examine some examples of a word of knowledge in the Bible, I have listed a few from the Old Testament and the New Testament.

Old Testament:

- 1 Samuel 3:10-14
- 1 Samuel 10:17-23
- 1 Kings 19:11-18
- 2 Kings 5:20-27
- 2 Kings 6:8-23

New Testament:

- Luke 2:25-26
- John 1:29-34
- John 6:60-61
- John 13:38
- Acts 5:1-11

Hosea 4:6a reminds us that God's people are destroyed for lack of knowledge. We most assuredly need the gift of the word of knowledge operating in our lives and churches today!

The word of wisdom is a flash of inspiration. It is a supernatural revelation sufficient for the occasion of the wisdom or purpose of God. It is the wisdom needed to meet a particular situation, answer a particular question, or utilize a particular piece of information.

Once again, it is vital to consider what the word of wisdom is and is not:

- It is not natural wisdom.
- It is not the wisdom gained from academic achievement.
- It is not wisdom gained from experience.
- It is not even the wisdom to understand the Bible.
- It is given as the Holy Spirit wills (1 Corinthians 12:11).
- It is given for a specific need or situation.

A word of wisdom may be revealed to a believer in Christ in the same way that I have listed previously for the word of knowledge.

It is helpful to know that we can pray for wisdom, understanding, and knowledge. In Ephesians 1:17, Paul prayed for the spirit of wisdom and revelation. In Colossians 1:9, Paul asked God to fill the believers in the church in Colosse with the knowledge of His will in all wisdom and spiritual understanding.

The following are examples of a word of wisdom found in the Old Testament and the New Testament:

Old Testament:

- Genesis 6:13-21
- Genesis 41:33 with Acts 7:10
- Exodus 28:3; 31:6 and 35:26
- Judges 7:5
- 2 Samuel 5:17-25

New Testament:

- Matthew 2:12-15
- Matthew 21:23-27
- Luke 20:22-26
- John 8:3-7
- Acts 27:23-26[i]

The Holy Spirit gift of discerning of spirits:

"The third gift along with the word of wisdom and word of knowledge that reveals something is the gift of discerning of spirits. It has a narrower range than the other two because it is limited to the spirit world.

Sometimes this gift has been called the gift of discernment which is in error. It is the gift of discerning of spirits. It is not the gift of discerning people; it is the gift of discerning of spirits. There is a huge difference.

From our study of scripture, we learn that there are four basic categories of spirits in the spirit world which are as follows:

- God - John 4:24
- Angels – Hebrews 1:14

- Evil spirits, deceiving spirits, and demons - Ephesians 6:12; 1 Timothy 4:1 and Revelation 16:14

- Man - Zechariah 12:1; 1 Corinthians 2:11a

A believer in Christ may be (1) operating under the inspiration of the Holy Spirit; or (2) expressing his or her own thoughts, feelings, and desires from his or her soul or spirit; or (3) allowing an alien spirit to oppress him or her and be bringing thoughts from that wrong spirit. An unbeliever in Christ may be completely possessed by an evil spirit. (Luke 8:26-39) The gift of discerning of spirits immediately reveals what is taking place. This gift is given to know what is in a person and to know the spirit that motivates him or her.

First, we need to define the word 'discern.' It is looking beyond the outward to the inward, literally, 'seeing right through', or 'insight.' In the gift of discerning of spirits, it means to distinguish between good and evil spiritual influences.

The following three verses are a sample of how the word 'discern' is used in the Bible:

- 2 Samuel 14:17 – 'And now your servant [the woman from Tekoa] says, 'May the word of my lord the king bring me rest, for my lord the king is like an angel of God in discerning good and evil. May the LORD your God be with you.' [NIV]

- 2 Samuel 19:35a – 'I [Barzillai the Gileadite] *am* today eighty years old. Can I discern between the good and bad?'

- Ezekiel 44:23 – 'And they [the priests] shall teach My people *the difference* between the holy and the unholy, and cause them to discern between the unclean and the clean.'

Some Biblical scholars believe that if there are no visions, (actually **seeing** the spirit), it is not the gift of discerning of spirits, but rather the gift of the word of knowledge in operation. They reason that if one is informed about a spirit, but has no vision of the spirit, he or she would not **discern** it. In some cases, a WORD comes first, then a vision follows.

Through the gift of discerning of spirits, we can discern the origin of certain actions, teachings, and circumstances that have been inspired by spiritual beings. It is the ability given by God to know what spirit is motivating a person or situation. The gift allows a believer to detect and identify spirits and provides supernatural revelation of the unseen spirit world, both good and evil. The real nature of this gift is knowing and judging – never guessing.

The gift of discerning of spirits is not a natural critical spirit, insight into human nature, human shrewdness, character reading, fault-finding, psychological insight, or even spiritual discernment. It is not a spiritual gift to uncover human failings. It is not the spirits of people who have died. It has nothing to do with spiritism or spiritualism. The spirits of departed human beings are not on this earth and to attempt to contact them is forbidden. [Deuteronomy 18:9-12]

Discerning of spirits is needed primarily to reveal the source of spirits. The first and most obvious function of this gift is to reveal the presence of evil spirits in the lives of people or churches. However, it also functions to evaluate the source of a prophetic message, a particular teaching, or some supernatural manifestation. The person functioning with this gift will be able to tell whether the source of the message or act is demonic, divine, or merely human. The gift of discerning of spirits enables a Christian to pick out the source of gifts and messages that truly come from God. Humans cannot be in contact with or understand the spiritual realm except by the power of God or the power of Satan. (1 Corinthians 2:14)

Although the gift has to do primarily with evil spirits, it also is the ability to detect the presence of the Holy Spirit. Visions, seeing Jesus or angels are also included in the discerning of spirits. If one only discerns evil spirits, then the Holy Spirit gift of discerning of spirits is not in operation.

Our natural discernment can be easily fooled. The gift of discerning of spirits is a means of protection from satanic deception. It is easy to confuse the words of the spirit of Satan with those of the Spirit of God. Satan counterfeits the beautiful works of God by creating an outward appearance that is similar to the real work of the Holy Spirit.

Satan is known as the deceiver [Revelation 12:9], the father of lies [John 8:44], and the serpent [Revelation 20:2]. All these titles signify the subtle, crafty deceptiveness which he uses to bring about evil whenever he can. Many times, his counterfeit is so plausible that one will be entirely deceived unless someone is present who functions with the supernatural gift of discerning of spirits. If demon activity was always so obviously reeking with evil and wicked intent, as we tend to imagine, there would no use for this gift of the Holy Spirit."[ii]

The following are examples of discerning of spirits found in the Old Testament and the New Testament:

Old Testament:

- Genesis 21:17-19

- Leviticus 19:31
- Deuteronomy 32:17
- Judges 13:3-7
- 1 Samuel 16:14-15, 23
- 1 Samuel 28:11-19
- 1 Kings 19:5-8
- 2 Kings 6:17
- 2 Chronicles 18:18-22
- Zechariah 3:1-2

New Testament:
- Matthew 1:20-21
- Matthew 16:23
- Luke 1:11-20; 26-38
- Luke 13:11, 16
- Acts 12:7-10
- Acts 13:9-11
- Acts 27:23-24
- 1 John 4:1"

Despite teachings to the contrary, God's people do receive dreams, visions, and prophetic words today. Here's a basic overview of this aspect of the revelatory realm:

1. God communicates through His prophets in one of two ways. "Let the prophet who has a dream tell the dream, but let him who has my word speak my word faithfully."[iii] As an aside, why would God want to stop communicating to us through prophets? Has He stopped speaking? Do people no longer need to hear from Him?

2. *Nāḇiy' prophet.* One of the ways God communicates to us is through a *nāḇiy'* prophet. "This word describes one who was raised up by God and, as such, could only proclaim that which the Lord gave him to say. A prophet could not contradict the Law of the Lord or speak from his own mind or heart."[iv] "I [God] will raise up for them a prophet [*nāḇiy'*] like you [Moses] from among their brothers. And I will put my words in his mouth, and he shall speak to them all that I command him."[v] Jeremiah was a *nāḇiy'* prophet, and he tried to refrain from giving the word of the Lord because doing so made him "a reproach and derision all day long."[vi] However, he could not refrain from giving the word of God.

> If I say, "I will not mention him,
>   or speak any more in his name,"
> there is in my heart as it were a burning fire
>   shut up in my bones,
> and I am weary with holding it in,
>   and I cannot.[vii]

3. *Hōzeh prophets.* Another way that God communicates to us is through a *hōzeh* or *chōzeh* prophet (hereinafter *hōzeh* prophet). "The word is "[a] masculine noun meaning a seer, prophet. . . . The word means one who sees or perceives; it is used in parallel with the participle of the verb that means literally to see, to perceive. . . . It appears that the participles of *hōzeh* and *rā'āh* function synonymously. But, terminology aside, a seer functioned the same as a prophet, who was moved by God and had divinely given insight."[viii] *Rā'āh* or *rō'eh* is "a verb meaning to see" and can "connote a spiritual observation and comprehension by means of seeing visions."[ix]

A prophet can function as both a *nāḇiy'* prophet and a *hōzeh* prophet. For example, Jeremiah functioned as both.

> But the Lord said to me,
>   "Do not say, 'I am only a youth';
>   for to all to whom I send you, you shall go,
>   and whatever I command you, you shall speak.
>   . . . .
>   declares the Lord."
> Then the Lord put forth His hand and touched my mouth, and the Lord said to me:
>   "Behold, I have put My words in your mouth.
>   . . . .

And the word of the LORD came to me, saying, "Jeremiah, what do you see?" And I said, "I see an almond branch." Then the LORD said to me, "You have seen well, for I am watching over my word to perform it."[x]

King David was assigned all three types of prophets.

Now the acts of King David, from first to last, are written in the Chronicles of Samuel the seer [*rā'āh*], and in the Chronicles of Nathan the prophet [*nābiy'*], and in the Chronicles of Gad the seer [*hōzeh*], with accounts of all his rule and his might and of the circumstances that came upon him and upon Israel and upon all the kingdoms of the countries.[xi]

4. **Examples of the ministry of prophets include the following:**

   a. **Rebuking someone for sin.**

   The LORD sent Nathan the prophet to David to tell him a story about a rich man who stole and prepared for eating a lamb that had been raised in the home of a poor man.[xii]

   Then David's anger was greatly kindled against the man, and he said to Nathan, "As the LORD lives, the man who has done this deserves to die, and he shall restore the lamb fourfold, because he did this thing, and because he had no pity."[xiii]

   Nathan then said to David "You are the man!" referring to David having Uriah the Hittite killed in battle in order to cover the sin of David's adultery with Bathsheba.[xiv]

   b. **Turning peoples' hearts to the LORD.**

   An angel appeared to Zechariah and told him that Elizabeth, his wife who was barren and advanced in years, would have a child, "[a]nd he [John the Baptist] will turn many of the children of Israel to the Lord their God."[xv]

   c. **Bringing people back into a covenant relationship with God.**

   And they abandoned the house of the LORD, the God of their fathers, and served the Asherim and the idols. And wrath came upon Judah and Jerusalem for this guilt of theirs. Yet he sent prophets among them to bring them back to the LORD. These testified against them, but they would not pay attention.[xvi]

   d. **Warning of what will occur in the future.**

   Now in these days prophets came down from Jerusalem to Antioch. And one of them named Agabus stood up and foretold by the Spirit that there would be a great famine over all the world (this took place in the days of Claudius). So the disciples determined, everyone according to his ability, to send relief to the brothers living in Judea. And they did so, sending it to the elders by the hand of Barnabas and Saul.[xvii]

e. Exhorting and strengthening the brethren.

And Judas and Silas, who were themselves prophets, encouraged and strengthened the brothers with many words.[xviii]

f. Giving divine direction.

Now there were in the church at Antioch prophets and teachers, Barnabas, Simeon who was called Niger, Lucius of Cyrene, Manaen a lifelong friend of Herod the tetrarch, and Saul. While they were worshiping the Lord and fasting, the Holy Spirit said, "Set apart for me Barnabas and Saul for the work to which I have called them." Then after fasting and praying they laid their hands on them and sent them off.[xix]

g. Speaking against sin; warning of judgment, and preaching about hope and renewal.

Then the LORD put out his hand and touched my mouth. And the LORD said to me,
> "Behold, I have put my words in your mouth.
> See, I have set you this day over nations and over kingdoms,
> to pluck up and to break down,
> to destroy and to overthrow,
> to build and to plant."[xx]

Jeremiah's message is threefold: (1) he must **pluck up** and **break down**, which refers to preaching against sin; (2) he must **destroy** and **overthrow**, which relates to messages concerning judgment; and (3) he must **build** and **plant**, which means he must preach about hope and renewal."[xxi]

All prophets do not have the same anointing or spiritual assignments. Some are called to prophesy to the people, some to persons in government, some to individuals, and some to geographic regions, mountains, land, rivers, etc. In addition, some receive prophecies more frequently than others. "Do not despise prophecies, but test everything; hold fast what is good."[xxii]

We are not to blindly accept what is prophesied. In church, "[l]et two or three prophets speak and let the others weigh what is said. If a revelation is made to another sitting there, let the first be silent. For you can all prophesy one by one, so that all may learn and all be encouraged, and the spirits of prophets are subject to prophets."[xxiii] A prophet may be male or female.[xxiv]

My personal prayer is that you will be enlightened, strengthened, and encouraged as you study this workbook and record what God, Jesus, and The Holy Spirit reveal to you. Time spent with Them along with reading and studying the Bible yields great dividends.

Please check out my new website: **www.sheilaeismann.com**

Also, if you would like to send an email or have questions about this workbook, my address is **sheila@sheilaeismann.com**. Thank you!

"The LORD bless you and keep you;
The LORD make His face shine upon you,
And be gracious to you;
The LORD lift up His countenance upon you,
And give you peace." (Numbers 6:24-26)

Prophetic Vision – 5 Standing Dominoes

March 4, 2022

Prophetic Visions

"Go West, young man, and grow up with the country," was the famous piece of advice that Horace Greeley, a New York newspaper editor, gave Josiah B. Grinnell in 1854. Since I grew up in the Mountain West, I didn't necessarily need the same suggestion. However, when heading west on my daily prayer walk on March 2, 2022, the Spirit realm opened, and I saw five standing dominoes. Suddenly, the scene switched to falling dominoes.

Nowadays, domino sets can be found in almost any color combination. The most common ones are still the white dominoes with black pips and black dominoes with white pips. An individual domino is named for the number of pips it has on each half of its face.

Dominoes

In the recent prophetic vision given to me, **each domino had one pip on the top half of its face.** Concerning the bottom half of the dominoes, the first domino had one pip on its bottom half, the second had two pips on its bottom half, the third had three pips on its bottom half, the fourth had four pips on its bottom half, and the fifth had five pips on its bottom half. (The above image is not exactly what I saw in the Spirit, but it will give you an idea of one pip on the top half of its face and the sequential numbers of pips on the bottom half.)

Since I'd never seen anything like this in the Spirit before, it startled me as no sooner did they appear than they started to fall. While I didn't see the entire set of 28 dominoes fall, I knew by revelation they had all fallen.

Next, I heard in the Spirit, "Falling like dominoes." I continued to wait upon the Holy Spirit for further revelation, but I only received the vision of the standing and fallen dominoes along with hearing the three words.

Serving God With Our Spiritual Gifts

Romans 12:6 reminds us, "Having then gifts differing according to the grace that is given to us, *let us use them:* if prophecy, *let us prophesy* in proportion to our faith."

When The Holy Spirit stops, we stop. We don't add to what we've seen or heard in the Spirit. This is one of the important safeguards within the prophetic realm.

Please revisit my previous weekly blog post of November 9, 2021, about exercising our spiritual gifts. Here's the weblink: https://sheilaeismann.com/give-receive/

Who's The Winner?

In a normal game of dominoes, the game ends as soon as a player has no more tiles left to play or when none of the other players can play a tile. If no player has managed to go out, the players add up the pips on their remaining dominoes. The winner is the player with the smallest total.

For a brief history of dominoes, here's a weblink: http://www.domino-play.com/History.htm

Revisiting what I heard in the Spirit on March 2nd, "Falling like dominoes," when this happens, it usually portends damage, defeat, or destruction. *******

1945-1991 marked a time of genuine global tension between our country and those of the Eastern Bloc region. The phraseology, "Falling like dominoes," was birthed during this time period.

The theory was that the major policies instituted by those in the Eastern Bloc area enabled them to quickly exploit and take over

weaker countries causing them to fall like a perfectly aligned row of dominoes.

When children are first learning to play the game of dominoes, they may try to line them up to see if they will suddenly fall in perfect alignment on a tabletop. However, what happened in the five decades following WWII in the Eastern Bloc region was no child's play.

Saving Face.

Significantly speaking as it pertains to the prophetic vision, each of the dominoes had one black pip on each face. This signals that each of the five is directly tied to the one in some manner. One is clearly in the driver's seat, in control, or calling the shots.

Dominoes have faces. Symbolisms for faces are someone's life or identity; heart; or revelation.

When the dominoes fall, whoever or whatever this vision represents will no longer be able to save face. They will have *lost face* as the old saying goes.

With face symbolizing someone's life or identity (when the dominoes fall), a person's life, reputation, or world standing would be damaged, defeated, or destroyed. *******

Plugging In The Prophetic Symbolism.

#1. Dominoes represent interconnectedness, repercussions, shock waves, playing games, spiritual momentum, spiritual repercussions, others falling, entertainment, partnerships, deception, chance, gambling, bluffing, and winners or losers. In this vision, there were no winners as all of the dominoes suddenly fell.

#2. Falling (the dominoes were falling) symbolize war, argument, or disagreement (having a falling out); an attack upon someone or something; spinning out of control; sinning; opposite of standing; ungodly; sinning; death; coming under the influence of someone or something; without counsel or support; and someone trying to trap another.

#3. The number five (five dominoes first appeared in the prophetic vision) is symbolic of grace; abundance; multi-tasking; redemption; favor; God's grace to man and man's responsibility. Since the dominoes fell, whatever this pertains to falls out of favor, grace, abundance, etc.

#4. The number two (the prophetic vision was received on 03/02/2022) represents division or separation; witness; testimony; association or agreement; partnership; support; interconnectedness; reward or multiplication; difference; and repetitive situation.

Stronger countries or people who take over weaker people or countries create an unfortunate, unjust, and repetitive situation.

Pharoah's Dreams.

While preparing this week's prophetic blog post, I'm reminded of Pharoah's dreams in Genesis Chapter 41. The Biblical symbolisms in these dreams were cows and heads of grain.

"Then it came to pass, at the end of two full years, that Pharaoh had a dream; and behold, he stood by the river. Suddenly there came up out of the river seven cows, fine looking and fat; and they fed in the meadow. Then behold, seven other cows came up after them out of the river, ugly and gaunt, and stood by the *other* cows on the bank of the river. And the ugly and gaunt cows ate up the seven fine looking and fat cows. So Pharaoh awoke. He slept and dreamed a second time; and suddenly seven heads of grain came up on one stalk, plump and good. Then behold, seven thin heads, blighted by the east wind, sprang up after them. And the seven thin heads devoured the seven plump and full heads. So Pharaoh awoke, and indeed, *it was* a dream." (Genesis 41:1-7)

In verses 25-27 of the same chapter, God gave Joseph the interpretation of Pharoah's troubling dreams.

Then Joseph said to Pharaoh, "The dreams of Pharaoh *are* one; God has shown Pharaoh what He *is* about to do: The seven good cows *are* seven years, and the seven good heads *are* seven years; the dreams *are* one. And the seven thin and ugly cows which came up after them *are* seven years, and the seven empty heads blighted by the east wind are seven years of famine." (Genesis 41:25-27)

In this powerful, prophetic dream, the cows and heads of grain represented 7 years.

Part of the joy of following God is learning about His revelatory realm as dreams, visions, and prophetic words are ultimately fulfilled.

Prophetic Insights For Daily Living.

A. How is your spirit stirred as you read and study this week's prophetic blog post?

_____
_____
_____
_____

If you like a challenging, prophetic puzzle, this one is for you!

B. Is there any significance to the dominoes being white rather than black or another color?

_____
_____
_____
_____

C. Who and/or what is the **one** pip on the top face of the domino?

_____
_____
_____

D. Much is happening around the globe as the kingdoms of this world continue to shake, rattle, and roll.

It could pertain to any of the following realms:

Governmental

Political

Financial

Religious

E. You may want to bookmark this particular blog post to watch for the fulfillment of the "Falling of Dominoes" just to see who and/or what the dominoes represent.

_____
_____
_____
_____

F. For those of you inquiring about having my weekly prophetic blog posts all in one handy-dandy place, please go to the **Book** page or tab on my website www.sheilaeismann.com. The *Prophetic Insights For Daily Living* series of workbooks contain all of my weekly blog posts and are a great way to study and learn about the revelatory realms of heaven, how God speaks and moves in our everyday lives, etc.

Each workbook contains ample room to answer questions, look up Biblical scriptures, learn about prophetic symbolism, and record your contemplations and how The Holy Spirit is teaching you or speaking to you. They are designed in calendar time frames of when I was given dreams, visions, and prophetic words and can be used as an independent study or in a group setting.

No matter what happens or how many dominoes fall, we can rest in the assurance that our God in heaven is always in control. No one or nothing is more powerful than He is. There's such comfort and peace in knowing this as we continue to pray for our country and the nations of our world.

"For dominion belongs to the LORD

And He rules over the nations." (Psalm 22:28 – NIV)

We have total peace from the Prince of Peace as promised in John 14:27, "Peace I leave with you, My peace I give to you; not as the world gives do I give to you. Let not your heart be troubled, neither let it be afraid."

Sheila Eismann, Prophetic Seer, Blogger, Author & Teacher, publishes her weekly blog posts endeavoring to encourage others through God's word. Her writings include teaching and instructions on how to apply prophetic insights for daily living.

Free The Fish

March 13, 2022

Prophetic Visions

As we daily seek the Lord to discern what's upon His heart, heavenly revelations can be quite intriguing and encouraging. In the most recent prophetic vision I received, The Holy Spirit zoomed in to an area beneath a well where rainbow trout were swimming in a circle but could not be accessed. I heard in the Spirit, "Free the fish."

In the second scene of this prophetic vision, I saw a man's work boot stomping down some soil to compact the dirt around the well. It was sort of like he was putting the finishing touches upon this evil intent.

Next, I heard, "Unstop the well." The reference to this wording can be found in the scriptural account of Isaac and Abimelech in Genesis 26:1-25. As this vision unfolded, I knew by revelation that the well had been stopped by human means.

When we consult the Biblical timeline in the book of Genesis, there was a famine in the land, so Isaac traveled to Gerar where he encountered Abimelech, king of the Philistines.

This particular Abimelech was a different man than the one mentioned in Genesis 20 as there's an approximate 100-plus year time difference. The easiest way to think of the various "Abimelechs" is like the different Roman Emperors who were called "Caesars", i.e., Caesar Augustus (Luke 2:1), and Claudius Caesar (Acts 11:28).

God had appeared to Isaac and instructed him to not go down to Egypt, but to stay put in the land of Gerar. This was in accordance with God's covenant with Abraham to give him the Promised Land (Genesis 12:1-3).

"Then Isaac sowed in that land [Gerar], and reaped in the same year a hundredfold; and the Lord blessed him. The man began to prosper, and continued prospering until he became very prosperous; for he had possessions of flocks and possessions of herds and a great number of servants. So the Philistines envied him. Now the Philistines had stopped up all the wells which his father's servants had dug in the days of Abraham his father, and they had filled them with earth." (Genesis 26:12-15)

Continuing to read through this chapter, we can readily sense why the Philistines, the original inhabitants of the land, seethed with envy and hatred toward Isaac. After all, in their eyes, a "squatter" plunked himself down on their land. Lo and behold, Isaac sowed in the land and reaped a 100-fold harvest in the same year all amid a famine! Small wonder they stopped up the wells that Abraham's servants had previously dug.

Names, Symbols, & Spirits.

(A)The word *Gerar* means lodging place. It was a Philistine town and district in what is today south-central Israel. Archaeological evidence points to the town having come into existence with the arrival of the Philistines at around 1200 BC and having been little more than a village until 800-700 BC.

https://www.google.com/search?q=what+is+the+meaning+of+the+town+Gerar&rlz=1C1CHBF_enUS800US801&oq=what+is+the+meaning+of+the+town+Gerar&aqs=chrome..69i57j33i22i29i30l4.5107j0j7&sourceid=chrome&ie=UTF-8

(B) Philistia or Philistine stands for migratory. (Genesis 10:14 and 21:32; and Psalm 60:8)

(C) Fish symbolize the souls of men; conversions (catching fish); humankind (potential believers); and spiritual food (the gospel of Jesus Christ).

(D) A well represents salvation or eternal life; The Holy Spirit; the human heart; God's word; the fountain of life -Jesus Christ; cleansing; the fear of the Lord; the voice of the righteous; Godly wisdom; and the cultural center of life.

(E) Beersheba mentioned in Genesis 21:14 means the well of the oath or well of seven. We don't know if this was exactly the 7th well that Isaac's servants dug where they were finally able to find water and settle peacefully.

(F) Genesis 26:14 tells us that the Philistines envied Isaac. There have been innumerable volumes written on the spirit of jealousy (Numbers 5:15) and its destructive consequences.

Are you familiar with the spirit of jealousy or have you read any books on this subject matter in the past?

Acts 12:1-3 indicates that it can be generational which is substantiated by the 100-plus years of the descendants of the Philistines stopping up the wells dug by Abraham's servants. With the Philistine meaning migratory, the spirit of jealousy often migrates.

Manifestations of this spirit are hate, cruelty, competition, anger, rage, revenge, and the horrible list goes on. For a water supply to be cut off endangering the lives of humans, animals, and vegetation, this spirit was alive and well during Isaac's time.

But the love of God and the workings of The Holy Spirit in our daily lives can and will prevail and overcome because the ultimate goal is to free the fish (souls of men). On June 28, 2021, I wrote of another "spiritual fish encounter."

The New, Big Bend In The River Of Your Life

https://sheilaeismann.com/millennials/

Prophetic Insights For Daily Living:

#1. Where's a present-day "Gerar" in your life?

_____
_____
_____
_____
_____
_____

#2. Look for the wells that have been stopped up as these are God-ordained opportunities for the exact days in which we are living.

_____
_____
_____
_____

#3. As a believer, we have the river of living water flowing from within us to touch the world and impact it for Jesus Christ. (John 7:38)

_____
_____
_____
_____

#4. God has readily prepared the heart soil of these people (souls of men – one of the symbols for fish) to receive the gospel.

_____
_____
_____
_____

#5. Perseverance is required for this project as we learn from reading the entire chapter of Genesis 26. Isaac continued to dig wells in the land until he found a place to finally settle. (2 Peter 1:5-9)

_____
_____
_____
_____

#6. Contending with the spirit of jealousy (evidenced by the Philistines) is not for the faint of heart, but the thing we must keep in mind is that he who wins souls is wise. (Proverbs 11:30)

"A true witness delivers souls." (Proverbs 14:25a)

_____
_____
_____
_____
_____

#7. God has a strategy and perfect timing to unstop every well to free the fish!

_____
_____
_____
_____

#8. As you ruminate upon the symbolisms for this prophetic vision, what other interpretations or spiritual thoughts come to mind? What is God leading you to do during the time of this great harvest to help bring souls into His kingdom?

_____

_____

_____

You will have to check the fishing regulations for your state to see the time frame in which you can legally fish, if applicable. However, in the kingdom of God, fishing season is open all year long!

Jesus's command to brothers Peter and Andrew still apply to all Christians today, "And Jesus, walking by the Sea of Galilee, saw two brothers, Simon called Peter, and Andrew his brother, casting a net into the sea; for they were fishermen. Then He said to them, 'Follow Me, and I will make you fishers of men.' They immediately left *their* nets and followed Him." (Matthew 4:18-20)

May God richly bless you as you follow Him and share the good news of the gospel of His Son, Jesus Christ of Nazareth. Sheila Eismann, Prophetic Seer, Blogger, Author & Teacher, publishes her weekly blog posts endeavoring to encourage others through God's word. Her writings include teaching and instructions on how to apply prophetic insights for daily living.

Soak, Seek, & Serve

March 18, 2022

Prophetic Visions

In the fictional world, there's a recommendation that the author creates a character, follows him or her around, and records what they hear, say, do, and so forth. Thus, the character takes on a life of its own and helps to drive the plot. I had a similar spiritual experience earlier this week wherein I saw a woman sitting in a hot tub. Next, I heard, "Soak, seek, & serve."

Soak.

When the woman turned on the various settings inside the hot tub, she added some drops of different essential oils. I saw all sorts of small, strange objects floating to the top such as species from the animal and plant kingdoms that I did not recognize. She didn't seem to be alarmed initially by them when she adjusted the controls inside the hot tub to increase the water coming in through the jets.

Just exactly how does a hot tub work? I'm so glad you asked!

"Hot tub jets have 3 components to them: water in, the air in, and an air mixture outlet.

"The hot tub's pump moves a pressurized stream of water through the filtration system's pipes, out the jet, and into the tub. Air is also mixed into this stream via a venturi, which is a small hole in the jet that water is directed through. This is referred to as the "Venturi effect."

https://poolonomics.com/how-hot-tubs-work/

I spotted a rectangular-shaped fish net on the side of the hot tub as this woman scooped up the objects and threw them over the side into a plastic bucket.

Seek.

I could hear praise and worship music in the background, and the longer it played, the more impurities floated to the top. It was at this point that she drew a metal rack close to her where her Bible was resting. There was a weighted length of plastic holding the pages open. Apparently, it was her custom to praise the Lord, read His Word, and pray during her soaking time.

Serve.

Next, I heard, "I'm calling you into a different branch of service in the kingdom of God." *Branch of service* made me think of the military in our country.

Have you recently felt like you're not quite sure where you fit or have lacked the opportunity to use your God-given gifts and talents? If so, this is an encouraging word for you!

Many were blessed within the past couple of weeks when viewing a newly married couple on nationwide cable tv sharing their testimony of how God is moving in their lives and the song The Holy Spirit downloaded to them. The bride had been given a dream as a forerunner to this sudden opportunity which was confirmed the day they appeared on the network.

After they married, this couple dedicated their lives anew to Jesus, anointed their musical instruments, sought the Lord in prayer, and waited upon Him. Within a few short months, He answered in a manner that exceeded their wildest expectations! "Now to Him who is able to do exceedingly abundantly above all that we ask or think, according to the power that works in us." (Ephesians 3:20)

Truth vs. Fiction.

At the opening of this prophetic blog post, I referred to creating characters when authoring fiction; however, this vision is not fictional. God's truth emerges in the hour when it's needed as a word in due season. (Proverbs 15:23)

The Key Reason For This Season.

The Lord impressed upon me that the key reason for Him calling us into different assignments for this season is directly tied to the forced, chaotic, and tumultuous movement of people around the globe. Granted, a very small percentage of them have relocated of their own free will, but this unrest and varied challenges pertain to the majority. As the people groups change, their spiritual needs especially do.

The City of Trees & A City of Refuge.

About a century and a half ago when the French fur trappers crossed the mountains and viewed our desert valley, they spotted a lot of trees growing, so they knew immediately there was a vital water source nearby.

Our capital city, Boise, is known as *Les Bois* or "The City of Trees." It's also referred to as a city of refuge. To that end, the refugee population has increased significantly, especially in the past couple of years.
It will take people responding to the new call of God in their lives to help minister to the newcomers, impart the love of Jesus, and give them the good news of the gospel.

As followers of Jesus, we have the anointing of The Holy Spirit expressed in Luke 4:18,

"The Spirit of the Lord is upon Me,
Because He has anointed Me
To preach the gospel to the poor;
He has sent Me to heal the brokenhearted,
To proclaim liberty to the captives
And recovery of sight to the blind,
To set at liberty those who are oppressed."

An Important Clarification.

It's important to remember to not feel guilty for where you have served or if you've just recently been called to a new assignment or spiritual sphere. This prophetic vision will confirm that for you. The enemy of our souls tries to inflict guilt and condemnation upon us, but God is the one Who infuses us with hope and encouragement through the power of His Holy Spirit. "Now may the God of hope fill you with all joy and peace in believing, that you may abound in hope by the power of the Holy Spirit." (Romans 15:13)

A good question for self-reflection would be, "How has the physical, spiritual, and geo-political landscape changed in my area?" Additional instruction and encouragement regarding spiritual assignments can be found when reading the following blog post "Our Sphere of Authority."

https://sheilaeismann.com/assignments/

Our Sphere of Authority

A Time To Wax Full & Not Wane.

This verbiage typically refers to the cycles of the moon wherein it waxes (grows fuller) and then wanes (grows thinner in appearance until you can no longer see it).

I hear the Spirit of the Lord saying, "It's time to wax full before Me, continue to wax full, and not wane."

If the moon is a faithful witness to its Creator (Psalm 89:37), how much more should we, as His unique creations, remain faithful to the call of God upon our lives?

A New Release Of Creative Art, Books, Metalwork, Woodwork, and Songs.

As you purpose in your heart to set aside time to soak, seek, and serve, God is going to impart to some of you a new release of creativity in the area of art, books, metalwork, woodwork, and songs.

This is not an exclusive list, but as the Creator of all good things, God will infuse you with creative ability which will help to draw people as you share the good news of the kingdom and the gospel of Jesus Christ.

Prophetic Insights For Daily Living:

1. Revisiting the things floating in the hot tub, could these possibly be?

Disappointments

Discouragements

Disillusionments

Distractions

What else would you add to this list?

_____
_____
_____

2. I'm being reminded by The Holy Spirit that the impurities (the objects floating in the hot tub in this prophetic vision) are going to drag us down in our new assignment if we don't get rid of them.

_____
_____
_____

3. Even if you're not able to travel, you can still participate. One woman that I know is on assignment for the Southern Sudanese people. Since she's unable to travel abroad, she has a paper map that she unfolds on her lap. As she lays her hands across the country, she prays in the Spirit and intercedes for this nation. I suggested she record the scriptures and revelatory downloads she's been given for them in her prophetic journal.

4. One of the things that I appreciate the most about God is that He is no respecter of persons. (Acts 10:34 and Romans 2:11) The playing field in the kingdom of God is a level one. The reason I'm mentioning this is because of the couple God allowed to be featured on national television to share their brief testimony and song of the Lord. What He's calling you to do is just as important. Obedience is the key.

5. Let us continue to pray for the areas of the world where people are experiencing such horrific situations daily.

Beloved brothers and sisters, stay the course with our precious Lord and Savior Jesus Christ as He has such good things in store for all of us. "And let us not grow weary while doing good, for in due season we shall reap if we do not lose heart." (Galatians 6:9)

Even if you don't own a hot tub or a bathtub, in the soaking and seeking, you'll receive your service assignment!

Sheila Eismann, Prophetic Seer, Blogger, Author & Teacher, publishes her weekly blog posts endeavoring to encourage others through God's word. Her writings include teaching and instructions on how to apply prophetic insights for daily living.

Please subscribe to receive new blog posts on her website at www.sheilaeismann.com. by clicking the "Subscribe" button in the far upper right-hand corner of her Home webpage.

A Key Over Tennessee

March 23, 2022

Prophetic Words

The Holy Spirit hovered over the state of Tennessee on Sunday, March 20, 2022, during our evening family prayer time. As we continued to pray and intercede, a key over Tennessee manifested.

Upon closer examination, this copper, skeleton-shaped key extended the full length of the state, even into the upper northeast corner of Bristol and Elizabethton. My attention was especially drawn to Elizabethton.

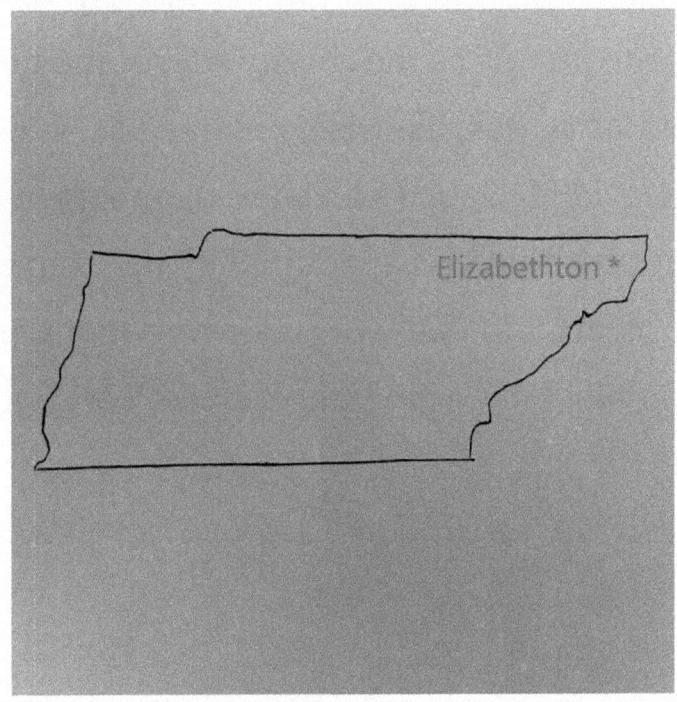

Elizabethton, Tennessee

Elizabethton is a city in, and the county seat of Carter County, Tennessee. It's the historical site of the first independent American government located west of both the Eastern Continental Divide and the original Thirteen Colonies.

<u>The City of Power.</u>

Elizabethton was first served by relatively inexpensive hydroelectric power during the early 1910s, leading to the popular "The City of Power" moniker.

Double Elizabeths.

Previously named "Tiptonville" in honor of Samuel Tipton while within the State of Franklin, the town was as the county seat of the newly minted Tennessee county of Carter was, likewise, renamed as "Elizabethton" by Landon Carter and David McNabb (who were members of a state committee to officially name the area that was appointed by the Tennessee General Assembly in 1796 to locate and name the county seat of Carter County) after their wives, Elizabeth MacLin Carter, and Elizabeth McNabb.

http://City of Elizabethton Bicentennial Historical Marker (hmdb.org)
https://www.hmdb.org/m.asp?m=192864

Drawing upon the name Elizabeth, we find:

"Literal Meaning: Consecrated to God

Suggested Character Quality: Consecrated One

Suggested Lifetime Scripture Verse: Psalm 119:34

"Give me understanding, and I shall keep Your law;
Indeed, I shall observe it with *my* whole heart."

Strong's H6942, *qadas,* pronounced *kaw-dash,* means to consecrate, sanctify, prepare, dedicate, be hallowed, be holy, be sanctified, and be separate.

A Biblical example of consecration appears in 2 Chronicles 26:16-18, "But when he (King Uzziah) was strong his heart was lifted up, to *his* destruction, for he transgressed against the Lord his God by entering the temple of the Lord to burn incense on the altar of incense. So Azariah the priest went in after him, and with him were eighty priests of the Lord— valiant men. And they withstood King Uzziah, and said to him, '*It is* not for you, Uzziah, to burn incense to the Lord, but for the priests, the sons of Aaron, who are **consecrated** to burn incense. Get out of the sanctuary, for you have trespassed! You *shall have* no honor from the Lord God.'" (Emphasis mine)

Prophetic Symbolisms.

#1. A key opens and shuts. It also represents access, opportunities, control, a way out of something, authority, revelation, knowledge, an important key player or item, love, God's will, prayer, signs and wonders, faith, and the power to bind and loose and lock or unlock.

"And I will give you the keys of the kingdom of heaven, and whatever you bind on earth will be bound in heaven, and whatever you loose on earth will be loosed in heaven." (Matthew 16:19)

It's important to note that this key stretched over the entire state.

#1A. Copper (key) symbolizes boldness, righteousness, strength, endurance, and judgment against the sin of disobedience.

#1B. The key was shaped like an old-fashioned skeleton key which is also dubbed a "passkey." It's a master key that has the serrated edge removed, so it can open innumerable locks, most commonly the warded lock, leaving only the basic part or design remaining.

#2. I received this prophetic vision and word on March 20, 2022, and 20 represents divine order, redemption, accountability, responsibility, waiting, expectancy, or the literal number of 20 such as 20 people or 20 of something specific.

The Consecrated Ones Hold The Copper Key.

I heard in the Spirit, "The consecrated ones (meaning of Elizabeth's name) hold the copper key."

Prophetic Insights For Daily Living.

A. Suffice it to say, every state in the United States and its people should be consecrated to the work of the Lord, but is there a particular emphasis upon the "Volunteer State" as evidenced by a key over Tennessee? It first became known with this slogan during the war of 1812 based on its prominent role of sending 1,500 volunteer soldiers.

"Your people *shall be* volunteers
In the day of Your power." (Psalm 110:3)

B. Since it's a copper key, watch for someone or a designated group of people soon emerging as standard-bearers exhibiting boldness, righteousness, strength, and endurance, all the while pronouncing judgment against sin of disobedience against God's moral laws.

_____

_____

_____

_____

C. There could be a play on words to the extent that someone residing within the state of Tennessee or the state collectively could unlock some "skeletons in someone's closet."

Will someone from the "Volunteer State" volunteer some valuable information?

_____

_____

_____

_____

"For there is nothing covered that will not be revealed, nor hidden that will not be known. Therefore whatever you have spoken in the dark will be heard in the light, and what you have spoken in the ear in inner rooms will be proclaimed on the housetops." (Luke 12:2-3)

D. Based upon the symbolism for the number twenty, watch for Tennessee to be instrumental in bringing divine order and redemption along with requiring accountability and responsibility. This is for the over-arching purpose(s) of redemption.

_____
_____
_____

E. At the start of my weekly prophetic blog post, I mentioned Bristol, Tennessee, which is known as the birthplace of country music, not to mention Nashville which launched the music business in our nation. A musical anointing still hovers over this state. Perhaps the music will be married up with the key, so to speak.

_____
_____
_____

F. After reading this word and ruminating upon it, how is your spirit stirred, or what has The Holy Spirit impressed upon you?

_____
_____
_____

A Call To Action.

For those living in the state of Tennessee, please take some time to pray into this prophetic word as you are more familiar with the spiritual, physical, and political climates at present.

Also, please leave a comment in the space provided for any updates or revelatory confirmations of this prophetic word.

Thank you, and may God continue to watch over all of us and the nations of the world during this dispensation of time.

"The Lord will watch over your coming and going both now and forevermore." (Psalm 121:8 – NIV)

Sheila Eismann, Prophetic Seer, Blogger, Author & Teacher, publishes her weekly blog posts endeavoring to encourage others through God's word. Her writings include teaching and instructions on how to apply prophetic insights for daily living.

Please subscribe to receive new blog posts on her website at www.sheilaeismann.com. by clicking the "Subscribe" button in the far upper right-hand corner of her Home webpage.

The Baker & The Five Loaves

March 30, 2022

Prophetic Teachings

A woman was standing inside her kitchen wearing a yellow, short-sleeved knit top and blue capris. Her clothing signaled spring or warm weather. Winter has passed, the flowers are starting to appear, and birds are singing happily. (Song of Solomon 2:11-13) The baker had just taken the five loaves of freshly baked bread from her oven and laid them on a board to cool. Watching this prophetic vision unfold reminded me of the Biblical account of Jesus feeding the 5,000 with the five loaves.

"After these things Jesus went over the Sea of Galilee, which is *the Sea* of Tiberias. Then a great multitude followed Him, because they saw His signs which He performed on those who were diseased. And Jesus went up on the mountain, and there He sat with His disciples.

Now the Passover, a feast of the Jews, was near. Then Jesus lifted up *His* eyes, and seeing a great multitude coming toward Him, He said to Philip, 'Where shall we buy bread, that these may eat?' But this He said to test him, for He Himself knew what He would do.

Philip answered Him, 'Two hundred denarii worth of bread is not sufficient for them, that every one of them may have a little.'

One of His disciples, Andrew, Simon Peter's brother, said to Him, 'There is a lad here who has five barley loaves and two small fish, but what are they among so many?'

Then Jesus said, 'Make the people sit down.' Now there was much grass in the place. So the men sat down, in number about five thousand. And Jesus took the loaves, and when He had given thanks He distributed *them* to the disciples, and the disciples to those sitting down; and likewise of the fish, as much as they wanted. So when they were filled, He said to His disciples, 'Gather up the fragments that remain, so that nothing is lost.' Therefore they gathered *them* up, and filled twelve baskets with the fragments of the five barley loaves which were left over by those who had eaten." (John 6:1-13)

An Important Progression

When reading the above passage of scripture, there's an important progression of which to take note:

An inherent spiritual test – John 6:6

The natural question (without eyes of faith) to a spiritual answer. A field worker during Jesus's earthly ministry was paid one denarius for a day's wage (Matthew 20:2). The 200 denarii spoken of by Philip would have been a little over a half year's wages – John 6:7

Jesus took the loaves and gave thanks – John 6:11

Jesus distributed the loaves to His disciples – John 6:11

The disciples distributed the five loaves and fish to those surrounding them – John 6:12

The progression goes from Jesus, our source of ALL things, to the disciples to the multitudes.

Fragments Are Never Lost

In John 6:13, Jesus instructed His disciples to gather up the fragments that remain, so that nothing is lost. They dutifully obeyed their master.

Do you ever feel like all you have are fragments to give to people?

Little is much when God is in it. We must not despise the day of small beginnings. (Zechariah 4:10)

Are you unsure of what your destiny is or that you're not doing anything in the kingdom of God?

Shekels

https://sheilaeismann.com/retirement/

One important clue regarding your destiny is to evaluate your passions and burdens. What are you passionate about in God's kingdom and what or who do you have a burden for in your life right now?

_____
_____
_____
_____

If you're not doing what you're supposed to be doing in the kingdom of God, The Holy Spirit will be faithful to show you, convict you, or communicate with you through the Bible, a dream, a vision, a prophetic word, or song, a trusted Christian minister or brother or sister, etc. This happened to the Apostle Paul on the Damascus Road during his dramatic, life-changing conversion. You can read all about it in Acts 9:1-8.

_____
_____
_____
_____

Oftentimes we can make this far more complicated than it actually is. In our country, we have such a tendency for hierarchy. God is no respecter of persons. You may be a caretaker right now for a family member or this may be your daytime, paying job. If this is what God is calling you to do, this is your kingdom work at this time as you can still manifest the fruit of the Spirit and share God's word throughout your everyday tasks.

Where we can run into trouble is through the "fans in the spiritual bleachers," so to speak, who continue to evaluate what we're doing and have no shortage of opinions.

Obviously, this is totally different than if a believer is walking in rebellion against God's word and His ways.

_____
_____
_____
_____

A Miracle of Multiplication

A miracle of multiplication coupled with a test of our faith in God is what the five loaves are really all about.

Bread symbolizes Jesus Christ; Communion (breaking bread); life (our physical lives are sustained with physical bread, and our spiritual lives are sustained with spiritual bread (the word of God), and words (our hearts and spirits feed on words).

Prophetic symbolisms for the number five are God's grace to man and man's responsibility; God's favor; redemption; abundance; and multi-tasking as evidenced by the five-fold ministry in Ephesians 4:11.

Plugging in the prophetic symbolisms for bread and the number five from above, God's grace and favor will rest upon you while multi-tasking to help feed the physically and spiritually hungry all for the purposes of redemption of mankind through His precious Son, Jesus Christ of Nazareth.

Invite someone for a meal and plan to share spiritual thoughts and the word of God with him or her.

_____
_____
_____
_____

Take note of your natural surroundings in which to launch a miracle of multiplication of the equivalent of your five loaves – John 6:8-10.

_____
_____
_____
_____

We're living and walking in a dispensation of time wherein the need for increase and multiplication will become more necessary.

Prophetic Insights For Daily Living

#1. To set the contextual stage for this chapter from the gospel of John, Herod Antipas, all the while seeking Jesus, ordered the beheading of John the Baptist which was obeyed by his henchmen (Matthew 14:1-12). This would have caused no small stir reaching far and wide. Further interest in Jesus had grown since the disciples had preached throughout Galilee. Anytime there's persecution, unrest, and food shortages, people's hearts are stirred to find peace. Jesus is our prince of peace. (Isaiah 9:6)

#2. Are we implementing the progression of John 6:6-12 of what Jesus has entrusted us to distribute to those around us? Everything we have comes from Him. So, if we follow the progression, we receive from Him, look to heaven and thank God for it, and disperse it to the multitudes. Jesus to us, His modern-day disciples, and them from us to the multitudes.

_____
_____
_____

#3. How do you think the miracle of the five loaves challenged the disciples in Jesus's day?

_____
_____

#4. What is the equivalent of your five loaves?

There's physical food and then there's spiritual food. After enduring 40 days and nights of fasting in the wilderness, Jesus refuted the devil's temptation by answering him from the word of God and quoting from Deuteronomy 8:3, "But He (Jesus) answered and said, 'It is written, *'Man shall not live by bread alone, but by every word that proceeds from the mouth of God.'"* (Matthew 4:4)

Maybe you live in a city of 8 million people in a 600-square-foot apartment on the 12th floor, and there's not even extra space for a small pot to plant some tomatoes. Perhaps you don't know how to cook or have much food on hand, and you just stop at the local deli before it closes on your way home from work to procure your evening meal.

But you have a 5-pound Bible on your bookshelf. Well, maybe not quite that heavy, but you get my drift! Don your walking shoes, head out to the highways and byways, and start sharing the good news of the gospel of Jesus Christ.

We used to live down in the desert 3 miles from an unincorporated town with a population of 55 people. This number of persons would still be included in the multitudes if that's the only human connection that we have.

#5. Notice the woman in the vision had not just mixed up the bread and set it on her counter to rise before she placed it inside the oven to cook the loaves.

The loaves were baked. What's baked into your spirit, body, mind, and soul? This is what you'll be distributing to and sharing with the multitude.

_____
_____
_____
_____

#6. Do you have faith to believe that God can use what small portion or fragments you might have to give to the multitudes? Fragments are never meant to be lost. They are intended to be multiplied for God's glory and daily use in His kingdom.

_____
_____
_____
_____

#7. I would encourage you to read slowly and carefully through John 6:1-13. Make a note of where The Holy Spirit stops you and record the specific things that He is downloading to you.

_____

_____

_____

_____

"But without faith *it is* impossible to please *Him,* for he who comes to God must believe that He is, and *that* He is a rewarder of those who diligently seek Him." (Hebrews 11:6)

Even if you don't like to bake, every day holds the possibility of miracles!

Sheila Eismann, Prophetic Seer, Blogger, Author & Teacher, publishes her weekly blog posts endeavoring to encourage others through God's word. Her writings include teaching and instructions on how to apply prophetic insights for daily living.

Please subscribe to receive new blog posts on her website at www.sheilaeismann.com. by clicking the "Subscribe" button in the far upper right-hand corner of her Home webpage.

Sheila Eismann

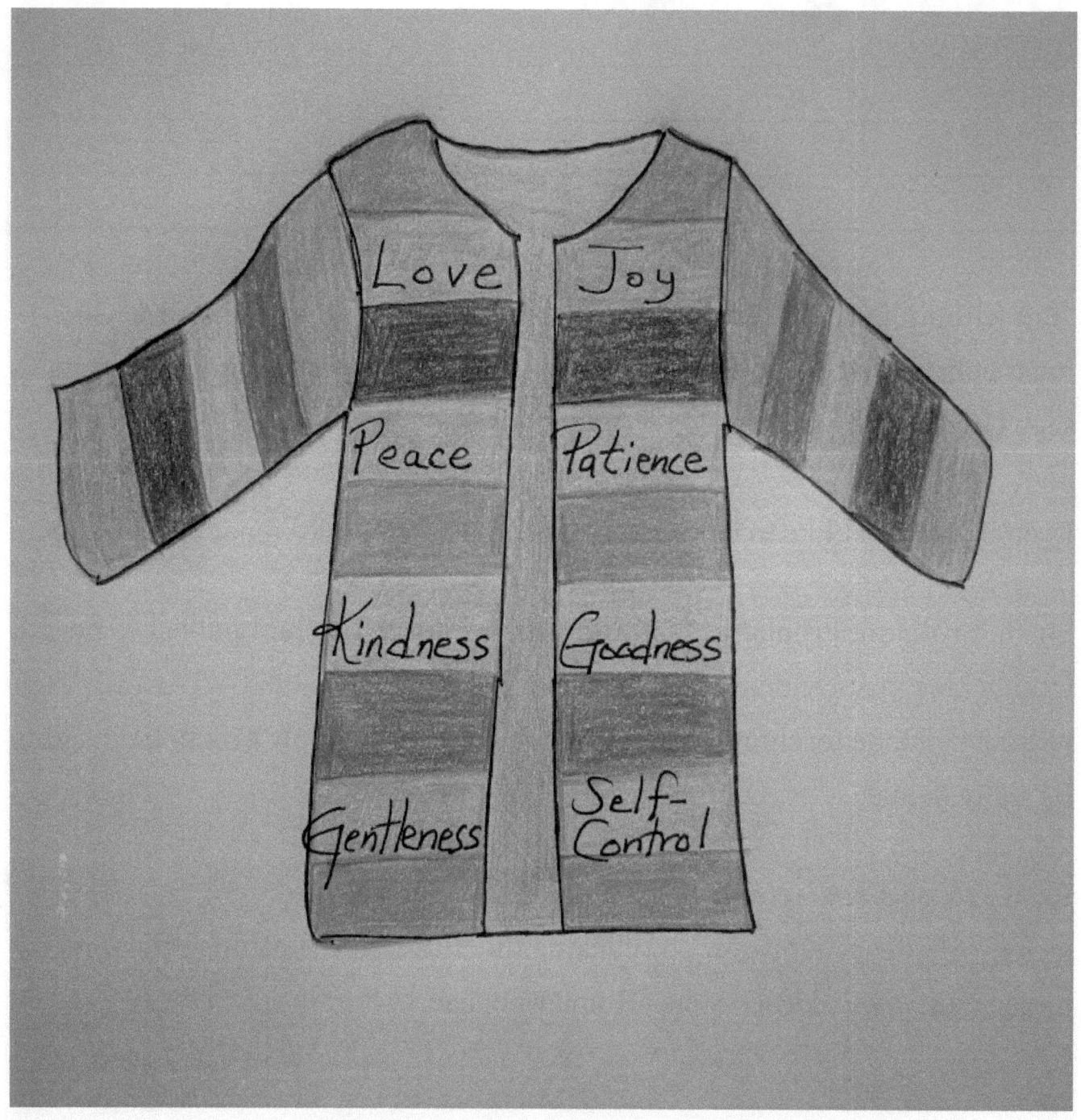

A Coat of Many Colors

April 6, 2022

Prophetic Visions

Viewing a child's artwork can bring such joy and refreshment to our souls! After recruiting some artistic help, "A Coat of Many Colors" was quickened unto me, and I immediately thought of Joseph's coat of many colors in the book of Genesis.

"Now Israel (Jacob) loved Joseph more than all his children, because he *was* the son of his old age. Also he made him a tunic of *many* colors." (Genesis 37:3)

Dreams From The Dream-Giver.

Joseph was a dreamer who was given two, powerful, prophetic dreams by God, the Dream-Giver. Unfortunately, this caused the spirit of jealousy (Numbers 5:14 and Genesis 37:11) to rear its ugly head and manifest in Joseph's brothers. Consequently, they stripped him of his coat of many colors and threw him into an empty cistern.

The wicked plot continues as Joseph's brothers fished him out of the cistern and sold him for 20 shekels to the Midianite merchants who took him to Egypt.

To cover up their dirty deed, the band of brothers took Joseph's once beautiful tunic and dipped it into goat's blood to take back to their father in the land of Canaan. They peddled their concocted story to Jacob which caused him to plummet into severe mourning.

Meanwhile back on the trading route, the Midianites sold Joseph to Potiphar, one of Pharaoh's officials.

As we continue to follow Joseph's life throughout chapters 39-45 of the book of Genesis, we find that Joseph went through many trials and tribulations, but ultimately, he rose to power as the second most important official in all of Egypt during a severe famine.

Since God's ways and thoughts are higher than ours, He used this whole series of events over many years to save Joseph's family which became the core of the nation of Israel. What the enemy meant for evil, God intended for good. (Genesis 50:20)

Our Coat of Many Colors.

There's another mention of a robe of sorts in the Bible that Samuel's mother, Hannah, made for him annually.

"Moreover his mother used to make him a little robe, and bring *it* to him year by year when she came up with her husband to offer the yearly sacrifice." (1 Samuel 2:19)

Until receiving this recent prophetic vision, I'd never really thought about the equivalent of a modern-day coat of many colors.

What manifested in the Spirit was the wording added to the various stripes on the featured colored drawing of a coat of many colors.

In addition to the fruit of the Spirit mentioned in Galatians 5:22, the other words which had been embroidered on the colored sections of the coat were:

Compassion

Forgiveness

Humility

Put On The Lord Jesus Christ.

In the Apostle Paul's letter to the church in Rome, he instructed the Christian converts and believers to put on the Lord Jesus Christ.

"And *do* this, knowing the time, that now *it is* high time to awake out of sleep; for now our salvation *is* nearer than when we *first* believed. The night is far spent, the day is at hand. Therefore let us cast off the works of darkness, and let us put on the armor of light. Let us walk properly, as in the day, not in revelry and drunkenness, not in lewdness and lust, not in strife and envy. But put on the Lord Jesus Christ, and make no provision for the flesh, to *fulfill its* lusts." (Romans 13:11-14)

Back to the coat of many colors that I saw in the Spirit, the fruit of the Spirit was embroidered on the front of it which is such a great reminder to make no provision for the flesh.

Just as the coat is made from a pattern, when we put on the Lord Jesus Christ, we make Him the pattern for our lives and follow His commands in the Bible.

The whole coat of many colors speaks to the analogy of allowing our character to be conformed to the image of our Lord and Savior, Jesus Christ, especially when we are out and about among people. A vivid-colored coat catches the eye of most people, some of whom may be drawn to it.

A Wardrobe Check.

When writing to the New Testament church at Colosse, the Apostle Paul encouraged believers regarding a wardrobe check, of sorts.

"Therefore, as *the* elect of God, holy and beloved, put on tender mercies, kindness, humility, meekness, longsuffering; bearing with one another, and forgiving one another, if anyone has a complaint against another; even as Christ forgave you, so you also *must do*. But above all these things put on love, which is the bond of perfection." (Colossians 3:12-14)

While we may not think of Christlike attributes, daily living, and character as items of clothing, the above verses paint a very vivid word picture to serve as a great reminder.

About a year ago, I posted a blog with a similar theme which I invite you to check out here:

https://sheilaeismann.com/wardrobe-check/

Strength, Dignity & Laughter In Your Future

A coat is an outer garment that people typically see when they first notice us. It makes an impression and covers what we are wearing under it. Our actions can be the opposite as they reveal what's in our hearts.

We can only put on the coat containing love, joy, peace, patience, kindness, goodness, faithfulness, gentleness, and self-control if that's what's in our hearts. (Matthew 12:35)

Our walk is how we live our lives, and we should walk worthy of the Lord, fully pleasing Him, being fruitful in every good work, and increasing in the knowledge of God. (Colossians 1:10)

Prophetic Insights For Daily Living.

#1. The story of Joseph's life reminds us that we must go through many tribulations to enter the kingdom of God.

"And when they (Paul and Barnabas) had preached the gospel to that city and made many disciples, they returned to Lystra, Iconium, and Antioch, strengthening the souls of the disciples, exhorting *them* to continue in the faith, and *saying,* 'We must through many tribulations enter the kingdom of God.'" (Acts 14:21-22)

As you reflect upon your life, can you relate to any aspects of Joseph's rejection, trials, & tribulations, or those of anyone else mentioned in the Bible? If so, it's important to give thanks to God for helping you through those challenging times.

_____
_____
_____
_____
_____
_____

#2. God is our dream-giver. What dreams has He given to you? Have all of them been fulfilled? If not, continue to pray into them and wait upon Him. A lot of time passed in Joseph's life before the dreams that God had given to him were brought to completion.

_____
_____
_____
_____
_____

#3. Just like we are reminded to put on the armor of God daily which is listed in Ephesians 6:10-18, we can wear our coat, shirt, sweater, or top of many colors where ever we go each day.

_____
_____
_____
_____

#4. Upon examining our coat of many colors, if we see that any of the colored fabric stripes need to be repaired, this is an indication of which fruit of the Spirit or character of Christ we need to have mended in our lives. We can do this with The Holy Spirit's help as we yield to Him.

#5. When praying into this prophetic vision and teaching, what additional embroidered words appear on your coat of many colors?

#6. Meditating upon the wording *put on the Lord Jesus Christ*, how does this speak to you?

Fellow saints, don your coat of many colors! We are blessed mightily by the Lord Jesus Christ every moment of each day. With every breath and step, we have the glorious opportunity to serve Him, praise Him, and love others through Him.

Sheila Eismann, Prophetic Seer, Blogger, Author & Teacher, publishes her weekly blog posts endeavoring to encourage others through God's word. Her writings include teaching and instructions on how to apply prophetic insights for daily living. Please subscribe to receive new blog posts on her website at www.sheilaeismann.com. by clicking the "Subscribe" button in the far upper right-hand corner of her Home webpage.

Holy Week Gifts

April 13, 2022

Prophetic Teachings

Christians worldwide are celebrating each day between Palm Sunday and Resurrection Sunday. My Spirit has been stirred and challenged by the theme of Holy Week Gifts.

Rewind the tape to A.D. 30 in the city of Jerusalem where most residents would probably not have realized it would be Jesus's last week on earth.

A Highly Compressed Seven Days.

Day 1 – Palm Sunday began with Jesus's triumphal entry into Jerusalem on the first day of the Hebrew week. To fulfill the prophecy of Zechariah 9:9, the crowd shouted "Hosanna to the son of David" in accordance with Psalm 118:25-26, as they laid their clothing and palm branches on the road. (Matthew 21:1-9)

Their holy week gifts would have been their items of clothing, palm branches, and their praise and adoration for Jesus.

Jesus went to the temple only to discover the traders and money changers who made an egregious profit from the sale of their wares. As He overturned their tables, Jesus chastised them accordingly, "And He (Jesus) said to them, 'It is written, 'My house shall be called a house of prayer,' but you have made it a 'den of thieves.'" (Matthew 21:13)

Day 2 – During the time that Jesus returned to the city the next morning, He cursed the fig tree for bearing no fruit. Jesus's words regarding faith still ring true today, "So Jesus answered and said to them (His disciples), 'Assuredly, I say to you, if you have faith and do not doubt, you will not only do what was done to the fig tree, but also if you say to this mountain, 'Be removed and be cast into the sea,' it will be done. And whatever things you ask in prayer, believing, you will receive.'" (Matthew 21:21-22)

Day 3 – "Tension Tuesday" began with Jesus being confronted in the temple by the chief priests and elders regarding His authority.
Standing on the Mount of Olives, Jesus taught on the Parable of the Two Sons and The Wicked Vinedressers. (Matthew 23:1-24; 31 and 36-44) He issued warnings about the Pharisees, futuristic predictions regarding the destruction of the temple, and His second return.

One of the most significant gifts ever recorded as being bestowed upon Jesus, and appropriately during holy week, took place during His stay in Bethany.

"And when Jesus was in Bethany at the house of Simon the leper, a woman came to Him having an alabaster flask of very costly fragrant oil, and she poured *it* on His head as He sat *at the table*. But when His disciples saw *it*, they were indignant, saying, 'Why this waste? For this fragrant oil might have been sold for much and given to *the* poor.'

"But when Jesus was aware of *it*, He said to them, 'Why do you trouble the woman? For she has done a good work for Me. For you have the poor with you always, but Me you do not have always. For in pouring this fragrant oil on My body, she did *it* for My burial. Assuredly, I say to you, wherever this gospel is preached in the whole world, what this woman has done will also be told as a memorial to her.'" (Matthew 26:6-13)

Day 4 – The Bible instructs us that there's nothing hidden that will not be revealed sometime in the future. (Luke 8:17) The deadly plot against Jesus was hatched on this day when Judas, the betrayer, went to the chief priests and cut a deal with them. (Matthew 26:14-16)

Day 5 – On the first day of the Feast of Unleavened Bread Jesus celebrated the Passover with His disciples; ate His last supper with them and instituted our present-day practice of communion; predicted the Apostle Peter's denial of Him; offered His agonizing prayer in the Garden of Gethsemane; was arrested and faced a trial before the Sanhedrin (the equivalent of the Jewish Supreme Court in those days). (Matthew 26:17-68)

In September 2020, one of my blog posts addressed the subject of communion. How blessed we are to be able to continue this all-important spiritual practice until Jesus returns.

https://sheilaeismann.com/clues-in-communion-bread/

The Four Communions

Day 6 – This was the most horrible day in all of recorded human history, but the most necessary one. Jesus carried his cross to Golgotha, "The Place of the Skull," to be crucified along with two other prisoners. His body was laid to rest in Joseph's tomb where it lay throughout the Sabbath. (Matthew 27:1-66)

Day 7 – Jesus is risen!

"Now after the Sabbath, as the first *day* of the week began to dawn, Mary Magdalene and the other Mary came to see the tomb. And behold, there was a great earthquake; for an angel of the Lord descended from heaven, and came and rolled back the stone from the door, and sat on it. His countenance was like lightning, and his clothing as white as snow. And the guards shook for fear of him, and became like dead *men*.

"But the angel answered and said to the women, 'Do not be afraid, for I know that you seek Jesus who was crucified. He is not here; for He is risen, as He said. Come, see the place where the Lord lay. And go quickly and tell His disciples that He is risen from the dead, and indeed He is going before you into Galilee; there you will see Him. Behold, I have told you.'

"So they went out quickly from the tomb with fear and great joy, and ran to bring His disciples word." (Matthew 28:1-18)

A Heart-Wrenching Week.

Suffice it to say, just reading about the last week of Jesus's earthly life stirs up profound emotion within our hearts and spirits.

God's perfect plan for the redemption of mankind was fulfilled in the birth and death of His beloved one and only Son, Jesus Christ, Who gave His life as the ultimate gift, so believers could spend eternity with Him.

<u>Prophetic Insights For Daily Living.</u>

#1. As you read this week's blog post and the accompanying scriptures, how are your heart and spirit stirred, challenged, and renewed?

_____
_____
_____
_____

#2. Jesus gave the most important gift of all time when He willingly and obediently died on the cross for the sins of all humanity.

_____
_____
_____
_____

#3. What are some holy week gifts you feel led to offer to Jesus? Sometimes, these are not tangible gifts such as monetary offerings or helping mankind in whatever manner He instructs.

_____
_____
_____
_____

Perhaps our resurrected Lord Jesus is asking you for your gift of obedience, faith, love, kindness, or acceptance of Him as your personal Lord and Savior, so your name will be written in the Lamb's book of life.

#4. I would like to encourage you to not allow the opinions of others to stir up discouragement in your life as to the offering of your holy week gifts. Revisiting the Biblical account of when Jesus was in Bethany at the house of Simon the leper, a woman came to Him having an alabaster flask of very costly fragrant oil which she poured on Jesus's head while he sat at the table. (Matthew 26:6-9)

Even Jesus's very own disciples became indignant concerning this woman's gift.

Jesus will be well pleased with whatever valuable gift we "pour out" to one another.

If you look carefully at the image accompanying this week's blog post, you can see the reflection of the "synthetic spikenard" from the green bottle onto the white cloth.

Here's a link with some additional information regarding spikenard: https://www.claiborneprogress.net/2019/08/05/spikenard-connecting-our-mountains-with-the-bible/#:~:text=It%20was%20used%20as%20an,His%20crucifixion%20was%20highly%20symbolic.

When we pour ourselves out to others, there's a direct reflection of who we are in Jesus our Lord.

#5. Holy Week Gifts are intended to be very costly. Take some time to meditate upon Jesus's gift of His life. After spending some serious, concentrated time in prayer, the Holy Spirit will reveal to us what our gift(s) should be. For instance, it may be an even greater degree or measure of obedience than what we are already exercising. No price tag can be placed upon spiritual treasures.

_____

_____

_____

Jesus, thank You that your precious blood has cleansed us, delivered us, set us free, and saved us. (Matthew 26:28, Ephesians 1:7, Colossians 1:20, Hebrews 9:14, and 1 John 1:7).

May we be a blessing as we share the good news of the power of Your blood to others who need what we have received! In Your mighty name, we pray, Amen.

Sheila Eismann, Prophetic Seer, Blogger, Author & Teacher, publishes her weekly blog posts endeavoring to encourage others through God's word. Her writings include teaching and instructions on how to apply prophetic insights for daily living. Please subscribe to receive new blog posts on her website at www.sheilaeismann.com by clicking the "Subscribe" button in the far upper right-hand corner of her Home webpage.

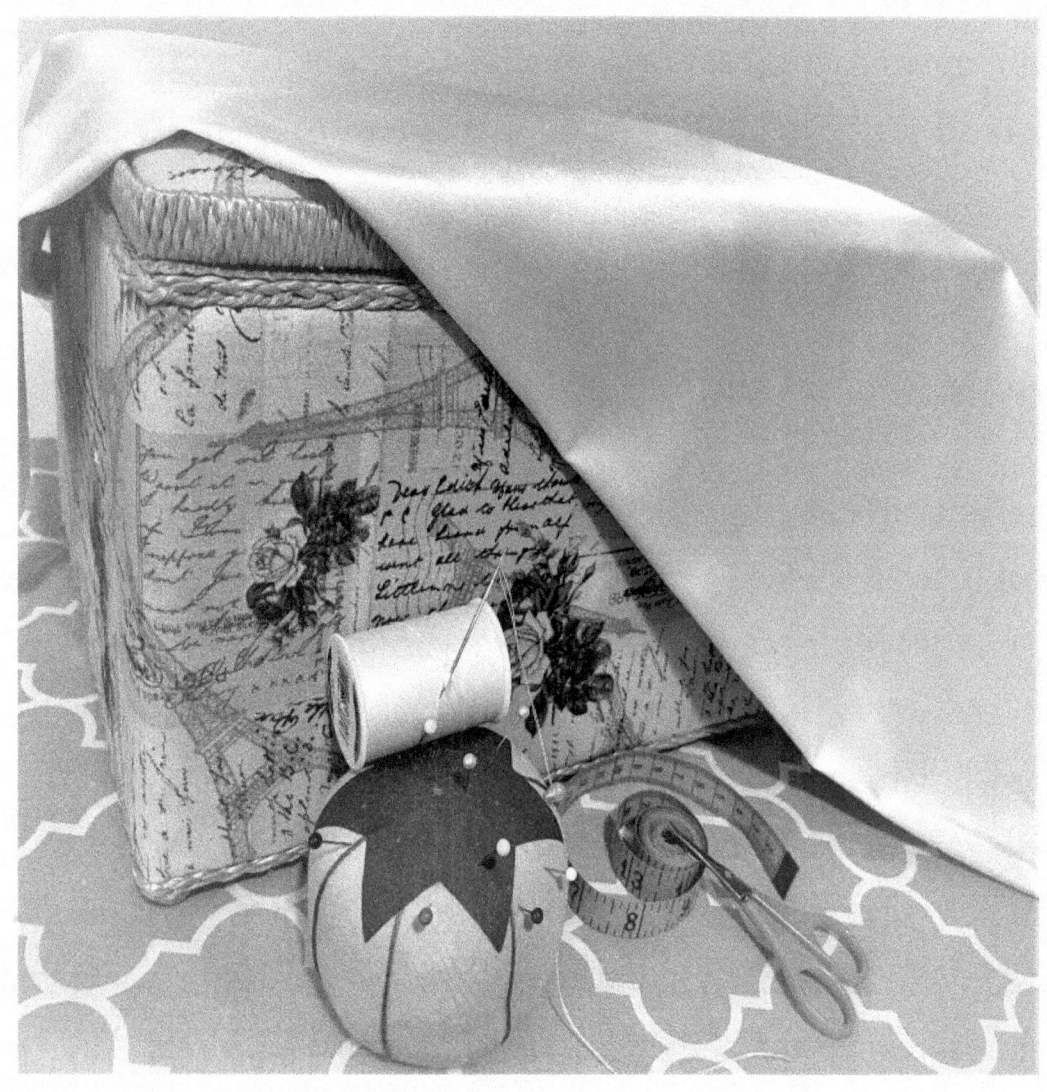

An Adjustment To Your Spiritual Wedding Garment

April 20, 2022

Prophetic Visions

The supernatural, Spirit realm is never silent nor dull. While preparing for our annual Christ in the Passover Seder Friday evening, April 15, 2022, the Spirit realm opened, and I saw a seamstress working on white satin fabric. I heard the Lord say, "I'm making an adjustment to your spiritual wedding garment."

Also, I knew by prophetic revelation this statement pertained to all Christian believers in Jesus Christ and the upcoming Wedding Feast.

"And Jesus answered and spoke to them again by parables and said: The kingdom of heaven is like a certain king who arranged a marriage for his son, and sent out his servants to call those who were invited to the wedding; and they were not willing to come. Again, he sent out other servants, saying, 'Tell those who are invited, 'See, I have prepared my dinner; my oxen and fatted cattle *are* killed, and all things *are* ready. Come to the wedding.' But they made light of it and went their ways, one to his own farm, another to his business. And the rest seized his servants, treated *them* spitefully, and killed *them*. But when the king heard *about it,* he was furious. And he sent out his armies, destroyed those murderers, and burned up their city. Then he said to his servants, 'The wedding is ready, but those who were invited were not worthy. Therefore go into the highways, and as many as you find, invite to the wedding.' So those servants went out into the highways and gathered together all whom they found, both bad and good. And the wedding *hall* was filled with guests.

"But when the king came in to see the guests, he saw a man there who did not have on a wedding garment. So he said to him, 'Friend, how did you come in here without a wedding garment?' And he was speechless. Then the king said to the servants, 'Bind him hand and foot, take him away, and cast *him* into outer darkness; there will be weeping and gnashing of teeth.'

"For many are called, but few *are* chosen." (Matthew 22:1-14)

On January 16 of this year, my weekly prophetic blog post addressed the subject of the future Wedding Feast spoken of in Matthew 22:1-14 and the Parable of the Great Supper in Luke 14:15-24.

I would encourage you to take the time to read my blog, and the accompanying scriptures, and ponder them in light of your all-important future.

https://sheilaeismann.com/the-most-important-wedding/

Wedding Hall

The Reason For The Spiritual Adjustment To Your Wedding Garment.

My curiosity was definitely piqued as I sought the Lord regarding what I'd heard Him say. His answer was not what I expected.

The reason for the adjustment was due to spiritual growth as a result of **persevering through trials and tribulations.**

In this recent prophetic vision and word, the specific area I saw being adjusted and expanded was the front bodice concentrating on the waist.

Prophetic symbols for waist are your spirit and truth. Obviously, there are spiritual truths and natural ones, with the most important being of the spiritual nature because, in the final wring-out, those are the only ones that will matter.

Under inspiration from The Holy Spirit of God, the Apostle Paul penned the following as part of the armor of God in Ephesians 6:14, "Stand therefore, having girded your waist with truth, having put on the breastplate of righteousness."

The truth of God's word is vital in an ever-changing, transformative society that is bent on defying it.

Fabric is symbolized as your life or your life's story. Would yours look a bit frayed at the moment? No worries! A call to Jesus will send heavenly help on its way.

There are many heavenly storehouses. The "Seamstress Storehouse" has no lack of fabric or sewing supplies.

Guarantees & Choices.

As the Apostle Paul and Barnabas continued on their missionary journey and after having had stones thrown at them and being dragged out of the city, they exhorted the disciples with these words, "We must through many tribulations enter the kingdom of God." (Acts 14:22)

Timothy was sent to the church at Thessalonica to help establish them along with the Apostle Paul's warning that they were appointed to affliction and would suffer tribulation. (1 Thessalonians 3:1-4)

The following poignant words penned while under house arrest in Rome still apply to each believer in Jesus Christ today,

"But what things were gain to me, these I have counted loss for Christ. Yet indeed I also count all things loss for the excellence of the knowledge of Christ Jesus my Lord, for whom I have suffered the loss of all things, and count them as rubbish, that I may gain Christ and be found in Him, not having my own righteousness, which *is* from the law, but that which *is* through faith in Christ, the righteousness which is from God by faith; that I may know Him and the power of His resurrection, and the fellowship of His sufferings, being conformed to His death, if, by any means, I may attain to the resurrection from the dead." (Philippians 3:7-11)

James, Jesus's half-brother, provides another look through a different spiritual lens.

"My brethren, count it all joy when you fall into various trials, knowing that the testing of your faith produces patience. But let patience have *its* perfect work, that you may be perfect and complete, lacking nothing." (James 1:2-4)

Have you or are you counting it all joy concerning your trials? What is the testing of your faith producing?

Tests and trials can be tremendous times of learning in God's classroom.

A Savvy Seamstress Works With Satin.

Have any of you in blogger-reader land ever sewed a garment or completed clothing alterations? I learned a great deal about satin fabrics when I sewed for weddings years ago. One must be careful to use pins, needles, and certain sewing notions that are fashioned exclusively for satin. The old saying, "A stitch in time saves nine" definitely applies to this situation. Regarding the plethora of types of fabrics on the market, satin is not as "forgiving" as some others such as cotton or cotton blends.

Even if you only know how to spell the word *sew* and have never taken a stitch in real life, thankfully, Jesus, our Bridegroom, will have our white robes (Revelation 7:9) ready for us when He calls us home to spend eternity with Him.

The white color and nature of the robes are because we will have been washed in the blood of the Lamb by which all of our sins are forgiven. (Revelation 7:14). Also, we have imputed righteousness granted to us because of our faith in Jesus Christ, the righteousness which is from God by faith. (Philippians 3:9)

Prophetic Insights For Daily Living.

#1. Reflecting upon your own life, when have you experienced the truest spiritual growth? Is it when life has been just sailing along without any interruptions, issues, challenges, or just the opposite of these?

_____
_____
_____

#2. With fabric representing your life's story, how will it end? Will you be in attendance at the Wedding Feast with Jesus?

_____
_____
_____

#3. In today's society, more emphasis is usually placed on the bride's attire for the wedding day as opposed to that of the groom. Viewing wedding photos of western culture, it appears that men wearing white suits on their special day is less prevalent than those of darker shades.

Both men and women will have white spiritual garments at the Wedding Supper of the Lamb.

#4. Recently, we were super blessed by a brief visit from a Christian evangelist from another continent. A portion of our conversation stemmed from the 1st chapter of the book of Galatians where the Apostle Paul reminded believers that there's only one true gospel. Today, there are many denominations, but there's still only one gospel.

"But I make known to you, brethren, that the gospel which was preached by me is **not** according to man. For I neither received it from **man**, nor was I taught *it,* but *it came* through the revelation of Jesus Christ." (Galatians 1:11-12) (Emphasis mine.)

Typically, the gospel preached in the cults originates with a **man** and his version thereof. The sad reality is those in the cults are going to find themselves in outer darkness where there's weeping and gnashing of teeth (Matthew 22:11-13) as they've fashioned their own wedding garments and scheduled their own wedding feasts.

May we be ever mindful to continue to pray for them that they would come to the saving knowledge of the truth before it's too late. (1Timothy 2:4) The false, works-based salvation(s) of the world do not come through the cross of the true Jesus Christ of Nazareth.

As you contemplate what your beautiful, spiritual wedding garment is going to look like, may your trials and tribulations lead you to a much closer relationship with God and become a launching pad for fantastic blessings in your life that you can share with others.

_____
_____
_____
_____

Sheila Eismann, Prophetic Seer, Blogger, Author & Teacher, publishes her weekly blog posts endeavoring to encourage others through God's word. Her writings include teaching and instructions on how to apply prophetic insights for daily living. Please subscribe to receive new blog posts on her website at www.sheilaeismann.com by clicking the "Subscribe" button in the far upper right-hand corner of her Home webpage.

T. F. T. ~ Today For Tomorrow

April 28, 2022

Prophetic Teachings

When we first met Robert, a country preacher from Alabama, he delivered an all-important one-liner that has stuck with me ever since. His exhortation is definitely for this day and hour as he proclaimed, "God prepares us today for what will happen tomorrow."

This week's prophetic blog post features an image of a wooden bridge leading into a forest. If someone had never traversed this path before but had decided he would like to travel it, there's really no way of knowing what lies ahead.

Unlike an unknown bridge and where it will lead, we can always rely upon the Lord to direct our steps if we will yield to Him and His ways.

"A man's heart plans his way,
But the Lord directs his steps." (Proverbs 16:9)

"In all your ways acknowledge Him, And He shall direct your paths." (Proverbs 3:6)

Taking A Page From A Fictional Book.

When penning fiction, there's an old adage that an author is typically a "plotter" or a "pantser" or perhaps a combination of both.

The *plotter* will generally outline his or her overall work of fiction from beginning to end while allowing for a little bit of elasticity in between. Enter the *pantser* who literally just flies by the seat of his or her pants without much planning until the last page is finished.

Applying the analogy above is sometimes how we navigate daily life. The saving grace is that we can always draw near to our Lord Jesus to help direct our steps to keep us on the narrow path which leads to eternal life.

"Enter by the narrow gate; for wide *is* the gate and broad *is* the way that leads to destruction, and there are many who go in by it. Because narrow *is* the gate and difficult *is* the way which leads to life, and there are few who find it." (Matthew 7:13-14)

Some Ways That God Shows Us Today How To Prepare For Tomorrow.

(A)His Word

"The prudent see danger and take refuge, but the simple keep going and pay the penalty." (Proverbs 22:3 – NIV)

"Go to the ant, you sluggard;
   consider its ways and be wise!
It has no commander,
   no overseer or ruler,
yet it stores its provisions in summer
   and gathers its food at harvest.
How long will you lie there, you sluggard?
   When will you get up from your sleep?

A little sleep, a little slumber,
   a little folding of the hands to rest—
and poverty will come on you like a thief
   and scarcity like an armed man." (Proverbs 6:6-11 – NIV)

What additional Bible verses would you add to this list?

_____
_____
_____

(B) An Authentic Prophetic Voice or Message

Despite what some present-day denominations teach, there are still prophets today and will continue to be until we all come to the unity of the faith and the knowledge of the Son of God.

"And He [Jesus] Himself gave some *to be* apostles, some prophets, some evangelists, and some pastors and teachers, for the equipping of the saints for the work of ministry, for the edifying of the body of Christ, till we all come to the unity of the faith and of the knowledge of the Son of God, to a perfect man, to the measure of the stature of the fullness of Christ." (Ephesians 4:11-13)

As the Old Testament Prophet, Amos, reminds us, "Surely the Lord God does nothing, unless He reveals His secret to His servants the prophets." (Amos 3:7)

This verse from Amos 3:7 can sometimes apply more on a global scale than a personal one, but the reason it's vital is because what happens worldwide affects us individually. We are starting to see that now more than ever before as the nations and continents continue to shake, bake, rattle, reel, and roll.

An Authentic New Testament Prophet or prophetic voice will have a proven track record of accurately bringing forth the word of the Lord in due season.

God didn't pour out all of His secrets just in the Old Testament. There are recorded New Testament prophecies (Acts 11:27-30), and He is still speaking today.

(C) A Dream Or Other Supernatural Encounter

In both the Old and New Testaments, God gave dreams to people to help forewarn them and supply wisdom and strategies.

A couple of examples are Pharoah's twice speak for double emphasis dreams in Genesis 41and Joseph's dream to protect baby Jesus in Matthew 2:13.

Does God supply you during the night seasons with prophetic dreams? If not, pray and ask Him to start giving them to you!

(D) Other Stirrings of The Holy Spirit

These would include hearing an audible voice from heaven, a spiritual song downloaded to your spirit, or just knowing something for certain within your heart. The Old Timey Saints referred to this as, "Knowing in your knower." The Holy Spirit is very creative, so there's no limit as to how He can minister to us.

(E) Nature – God's Creation

Our backyard is home to a gorgeous, majestic 55-foot-tall oak tree that sheds beaucoup acorns every fall. Suffice it to say, it's a squirrel's paradise. As I watch them scurry around to "squirrel away" their food for the winter, it's a great reminder for me to check the supplies in my pantry.

Can you think of other examples from God's creation that readily come to mind? If so, what are they, and how have you applied them to your life?

_____
_____
_____
_____
_____
_____

The One Who Does Not Change.

In a rapidly changing world, thankfully, there is One who never changes.

"Jesus Christ *is* the same yesterday, today, and forever. Do not be carried about with various and strange doctrines. For *it is* good that the heart be established by grace, not with foods which have not profited those who have been occupied with them." (Hebrews 13:8-9)

In Psalms 23 and 100:3, we are promised that the Lord is our shepherd Who takes such good care of us every day.

When our hearts are steadfast and trusting in Jesus, we will have no fear of bad news. (Psalm 112:5-9)

Living in Matthew 6:31-34 is a tall challenge but very possible as it's loaded with rich promises, "Therefore do not worry, saying, 'What shall we eat?' or 'What shall we drink?' or 'What shall we wear?' For after all these things the Gentiles seek. For your heavenly Father knows that you need all these things. But seek first the kingdom of God and His righteousness, and all these things shall be added to you." (Matthew 6:31-33)

Here are some additional verses for meditation: John 14:27 and Philippians 4:19.

The Most Important Preparation Today For Tomorrow.

We are definitely living in the days of the preparation of the Five Wise Virgins referenced in Matthew 25:1-13.

"Then the kingdom of heaven shall be likened to ten virgins who took their lamps and went out to meet the bridegroom. Now five of them were wise, and five *were* foolish. Those who *were* foolish took their lamps and took no oil with them, but the wise took oil in their vessels with their lamps. But while the bridegroom was delayed, they all slumbered and slept.

"And at midnight a cry was *heard:* 'Behold, the bridegroom is coming; go out to meet him!' Then all those virgins arose and trimmed their lamps. And the foolish said to the wise, 'Give us *some* of your oil, for our lamps are going out.' But the wise answered, saying, '*No,* lest there should not be enough for us and you; but go rather to those who sell, and buy for yourselves.' And while they went to buy, the bridegroom came, and those who were ready went in with him to the wedding; and the door was shut.

"Afterward the other virgins came also, saying, 'Lord, Lord, open to us!' But he answered and said, 'Assuredly, I say to you, I do not know you.'

"Watch therefore, for you know neither the day nor the hour in which the Son of Man is coming."

This parable can also be read and studied in Luke 12:35-40.

Prophetic Insights For Daily Living.

#1. Do you deem it important to be as prepared as you can be for what will happen tomorrow?

_____
_____
_____

#2. Has there been a time in your life when God has prepared you today for what was going to happen tomorrow? When was this, and what was the result? Were you thankful for the warning or advice ahead of time?

_____
_____
_____
_____
_____

#3. Are you spiritually prepared with your name written in the Lamb's Book of Life? This is the most important question each of us will answer during our earthly days. The words of the Apostle Peter still echo down through the chambers of time, "Therefore, brethren, be even more diligent to make your call and election sure, for if you do these things you will never stumble; for so an entrance will be supplied to you abundantly into the everlasting kingdom of our Lord and Savior Jesus Christ." (2 Peter 1:10-11)

_____
_____
_____
_____
_____

Additional scriptures to contemplate are Philippians 4:3, Hebrews 12:23, and Revelation 3:4-5, 13:8, 20:15, and 21:27.

#4. As you study and ponder the Parable of The Five Wise Virgins in Matthew 25:1-13, how do these scriptures speak to you? What vital instructions and warnings are being quickened unto you?

_____
_____
_____
_____
_____

#5. In March of 2021, my weekly blog post centered on the pitfalls and dangers of distractions that can sometimes enter our lives when God is preparing us today for what will happen tomorrow. Here's the link to scope it out: https://sheilaeismann.com/dangers-of-distractions/

Dangers of Distractions

My daddy, Fred, would oftentimes sit at the kitchen table inside our country house and listen to the song, "Don't worry, be happy!" Those words from my Sage Creek Farm days still resonate in my heart and spirit as I wait upon God to prepare me today for what will happen tomorrow.

"Be anxious for nothing, but in everything by prayer and supplication, with thanksgiving, let your requests be made known to God; and the peace of God, which surpasses all understanding, will guard your hearts and minds through Christ Jesus." (Philippians 4:6-7)

May all of you have a blessed week, and to have the peace of God, we have to trust Him with our entire future.

Sheila Eismann, Prophetic Seer, Blogger, Author & Teacher, publishes her weekly blog posts endeavoring to encourage others through God's word. Her writings include teaching and instructions on how to apply prophetic insights for daily living.

Please subscribe to receive new blog posts on her website at www.sheilaeismann.com. by clicking the "Subscribe" button in the far upper right-hand corner of her Home webpage.

Prophetic Dream ~ Norm, Debbie & The Dinner

May 3, 2022

Prophetic Dreams

Do you eagerly await the night season with great expectation as to what God will deliver into your spirit? I want to challenge you to set your dream bar higher than ever before. God's one-on-one communication is so personal and vital. When we are nestled in our beds, even when we don't have sugar plums dancing above our heads, is when our quieted spirits are prepared to receive. By way of encouragement, I would like to share a recent prophetic dream that was given to me involving Norm, Debbie, & the dinner.

Scene #1.

When the dream opened, I was scurrying around our house trying to get dinner fixed for Norm and Debbie. The reason for the haste was that all of this was totally unplanned yet urgent.

In my prophetic blog post last week, I alluded to a page taken from literary land where novelists are typically either dubbed a "plotter" or a "pantser." My siblings and I are far more *plotters* than *pantsers* in real life, so this genetic characteristic even trickled into dreamland. Would any of you in blogger-reader land be surprised to learn that all of us are married to "pantsers?" Opposites do attract, or at least that's what most folks opine.

Scene #2.

For some unexplainable reason in this dream, I was to place far more emphasis on preparing what Debbie wanted to eat as opposed to Norm.

Quite a bit of my time was spent looking through my cupboards, pantry, and refrigerator as I searched for just the right combination of foods and ingredients to be able to serve for this impromptu dinner.

Scene #3.

Before completing the meal and inviting our guests to sit down for dinner, it was dropped in my spirit to give them an offering of $1,000.00. While I appreciate this would be quite a hefty amount in real life, this is what I received in my prophetic dream. As I busied myself in our kitchen, I can remember thinking, "I've got to remember to give Norm and Debbie the check for $1,000.00."

End of dream.

On paper, this sounds like a short dream, but it went on for quite some time in the early morning hours. It ended before I served the meal or we sat down to dine.

Norm & Debbie In Real Life.

My husband and I first saw Norm in the late 1990s when he came to our valley on a speaking tour. At the time, he was not yet married to his wife, Debbie.

Norm is a pastor and prophetic teacher in real life who has ministered in different continents around the world throughout the decades.

We pray regularly for Norm, Debbie, and their ministry. In one sense, it was encouraging for me to receive a prophetic dream regarding some people for whom we are praying.

Decoding Prophetic Dreams.

********** Norm's character qualities and lifetime verse speak of a Northman who is strong and manly. Joshua 1:9, "Have I not commanded you? Be strong and of good courage; do not be afraid, nor be dismayed, for the Lord your God *is* with you wherever you go."

********** Debbie is the bee who is the seeking one. Jeremiah 29:13, "And you will seek Me and find *Me,* when you search for Me with all your heart."

God created bees that could not live unless they went out seeking daily sustenance.

Deborah, a prophetess, and judge in the Old Testament was a seeker of justice as she followed the Lord's command to deliver Israel from Jabin, king of the Canaanites. (Judges Chapters 4-5)

********** Since Norm and Debbie are married in real life, we "marry up" the meanings of their names. We are to remain strong in our Lord Jesus with no fear as we go about our daily lives seeking God knowing full well that He is our source, sustenance, and everything else we need when we need it.

********** In terms of prophetic symbolism, a dinner or food preparation sort of speaks for itself: spiritual nourishment, fellowship, intimacy, communion, relationship, provision, the heart, and serving the body of Christ.

In the dream, I spent quite a bit of time searching and seeking what I could prepare to feed Debbie for dinner.

********** The number 1,000 represents divine completeness and the glory of God. It's usually referenced in the book of Revelation as it relates to angels. "Then I looked, and I heard the voice of many angels around the throne, the living creatures, and the elders; and the number of them was ten thousand times ten thousand, and thousands of thousands." (Revelation 5:11)

In the dream, I was to present a freewill offering of $1,000.00 to Norm and Debbie for their ministry.

The Old Testament clearly outlines the various types of offerings that the Israelites were commanded to give.

Exodus 35:29 addresses a freewill offering. "The children of Israel brought a freewill offering to the Lord, all the men and women whose hearts were willing to bring *material* for all kinds of work which the Lord, by the hand of Moses, had commanded to be done."

Numbers 15:3 tells us this is a pleasing aroma to the Lord Who will bless it as it's given with no ulterior motive and from a generous heart and spirit.

We learn from Exodus 35:29 that the men and women had willing hearts. This is the key to any kind of freewill offering should the Lord move upon your heart to offer one sometime.

We don't "give to get" as some preachers profess. We do so because it's what we desire to do and want to follow the command of our Lord Jesus Christ. What do you think of the "give to get" philosophy?

_____
_____
_____
_____

When presenting the beatitudes, He instructed, "Give, and it will be given to you: good measure, pressed down, shaken together, and

running over will be put into your bosom. For with the same measure that you use, it will be measured back to you." (Luke 6:38)

In the Biblical context of Luke 6:27-38, these verses teach regarding giving and extending forgiveness, mercy, and grace to others just as God provides the same for us. Money doesn't even enter the picture or wording in Luke 6:38. It's paramount that we study the Bible to understand the whole counsel of God.

The Mercies of God

https://sheilaeismann.com/give-receive/

Prophetic Insights For Daily Living.

#1. Leaning into the lifetime scripture verse for Norm's name, have you been experiencing more fear or dismay of late as you glance at the headlines on your cell phone or sit down to watch the evening news?

_____
_____
_____
_____

As the Apostle Paul exhorted his young protégé, Timothy, "For God has not given us a spirit of fear, but of power and of love and of a sound mind". (2 Timothy 1:7)

Please notice from this verse that fear is a demonic spirit that is sent to harass and diminish us. As we walk daily with God, His Holy Spirit helps us to live in freedom without fear. "Now the Lord is the Spirit, and where the Spirit of the Lord is, there is freedom." (2 Corinthians 3:17 – NIV)

The antidote for the spirit of fear is the power of God through His Holy Spirit coupled with love and a sound mind since we have the mind of Christ.

"For *'who has known the mind of the Lord that he may instruct Him?'* But we have the mind of Christ." (1 Corinthians 2:16)

_____
_____
_____
_____

#2. Debbie's name speaks of bees who fly out every day seeking their sustenance. God desires that we draw near to Him every day for our spiritual sustenance and survival. This can be extremely challenging as the day runs into the night with the daily demands not to mention the fact that these days are not for the faint of heart.

_____
_____
_____
_____

#3. If the Lord leads you to do something impromptu to bless someone, does this throw you into a tizzy? Please keep in mind this could be even a small gesture that doesn't necessarily need to cost you anything except perhaps a little bit of your time.

_____
_____
_____

#4. How does this prophetic dream speak to you? Continue to ask the Lord for dreams to help guide, instruct and encourage you. If you're continuing to write in your prophetic journal, make sure to record your dreams and revelatory downloads, including scriptures, that you receive. Nothing is intended to be a substitute for the Word of God, but dreams can oftentimes confirm how God has been speaking to us through His word.

_____
_____
_____
_____

#5. One freewill offering that we can give every day to our Lord is the offering of praise unto Him. The sacrifice of praise is the offering of praise.

"Whoever offers praise glorifies Me;
And to him who orders *his* conduct *aright*
I will show the salvation of God." (Psalm 50:23)
"Therefore by Him let us continually offer the sacrifice of praise to God, that is, the fruit of *our* lips, giving thanks to His name." (Hebrews 13:15)

Here's wishing all of you mothers a very happy and blessed Mother's Day. As you proceed through your daily tasks, busy as a little bee, may you spread some encouragement everywhere you go. A kind word or a good deed may help to make someone's day so much better.

And for others who are not mothers ~~

"The Lord bless you and keep you;
The Lord make His face shine upon you,
And be gracious to you;
The Lord lift up His countenance upon you,
And give you peace." (Numbers 6:24-26)

Sheila Eismann, Prophetic Seer, Blogger, & Author, publishes her weekly blog posts endeavoring to encourage others through God's word. Her writings include teaching and instructions on how to apply prophetic insights for daily living. Please subscribe to receive new blog posts on her website at www.sheilaeismann.com. by clicking the "Subscribe" button in the far upper right-hand corner of her Home webpage.

Large & In Charge

May 12, 2022

Encouragement

Peering out our patio window, I watched as the snow pelted our freshly blooming lilacs. The thin branches swayed gently back and forth as the slight wind delivered the snowflakes to rest on top. In my creative mind, I could almost hear the lilacs crying out, "We're freezing and drooping under the weight of this fresh powdery outpouring from the sky!" Nodding my head up and down, I had to remind myself, "I know Who is large & in charge!"

"For He says to the snow, 'Fall *on* the earth';
Likewise to the gentle rain and the heavy rain of His strength." (Job 37:6)

This snowstorm surprise during the merry month of May is an extremely rare occurrence in our treasured Treasure Valley.

Heaven's Storehouses.

The book of Job in the Old Testament is a challenging read on a good day, not to mention on a stormy one! Toward the end of it, God reveals His omnipotence to Job in a mighty discourse delivered out of the whirlwind.

"Have you entered the storehouses of the snow or seen the storehouses of the hail?" (Job 38:22 – NIV)

If we ever need a reminder of Who is large & in charge, we can read slowly through every line of this chapter.

Here are a few other verses regarding Who controls the weather.

"When He utters His voice,

There is a multitude of waters in the heavens:

And He causes the vapors to ascend from the ends of the earth.

He makes lightning for the rain,

He brings the wind out of His treasuries." (Jeremiah 10:13)

"Who covers the heavens with clouds,

Who prepares rain for the earth,

Who makes grass to grow on the mountains." (Psalm 147:8)

"Fire and hail, snow and clouds;

Stormy wind, fulfilling His word." (Psalm 148:8)

Other supporting verses are Amos 4:7 and Zechariah 10:1.

Born of the Spirit.

"The wind blows where it wishes, and you hear the sound of it, but cannot tell where it comes from and where it goes. So is everyone who is born of the Spirit." (John 3:8)

The spiritual beauty and reassurance for Christian believers stems from our acceptance of Jesus Christ as our personal Lord and Savior and walking out our daily lives with Him.

Prophetic symbolism for snow is purity and a robe of righteousness as snow on the earth is like a robe of righteousness on an earthen vessel revealing

God's glory to mankind. We have the imputed righteousness of Jesus Christ. (Romans 4:6) The Trinity, God, His Son, Jesus Christ of Nazareth, and The Holy Spirit not only control everything but can handle anything that comes our way. What a relief it is to know this!

What A Difference A Day Can Make.

The following day, the sun-kissed lilacs were no longer drooping but had bounced back blessing us with their aromatic, spring scent.

Sun Kissed Lilacs

The petite, male finches, sporting their little red jackets, had emerged from their hiding place inside the blue finch birdhouse featured on the left side of the above photo. As they nibbled from the standing birdfeeder in our backyard, it was as if they didn't have a care in the world. Flitting from the feeder to another safe haven inside the boxwood bushes to the right of their birdhouse, they must also know Who is large & in charge.

Oh, the weighty & important lessons we can learn from nature and God's other creatures!

A Blessed Week of Surprises.

Not only was the May snowstorm a big surprise, but God always does exceedingly and abundantly above all that we ask or think. (Ephesians 3:20-21)

For my Mother's Day and Birthday week, God surprised me with a visit from all of my children! My cup of blessing and joy overflows.

Here's an inspiring blog post read from March 2021:

https://sheilaeismann.com/fill-your-cup-with-joy/

A Cup of Joy

<u>Prophetic Insights For Daily Living.</u>

#1. It can be so hard to fully trust God in every area of our lives, especially when the storms blow in unexpectedly. Have you learned to trust God for the duration of the storm?

_____
_____
_____
_____

#2. Just like the sunshine helped the lilacs to bounce back after the snowstorm, God's Son of Righteousness, Jesus Christ, helps us to bounce back after the storms of our lives.

_____
_____
_____
_____

#3. A really happy person is one who can enjoy the scenery when he or she has to take a detour.

"And whoever trusts in the Lord, happy *is* he." (Proverbs 16:20b)
Other comforting verses are Proverbs 3:5-6, Psalm 37:3-4, Isaiah 12:2, Matthew 6:25-34, and Luke 12:22-32.

_____
_____
_____
_____

#4. Just like the little male, red finches who had a safe place to shelter during the snowstorm, God provides a refuge for us at all times. A great suggestion is to memorize Psalm 91 which speaks of dwelling in the shelter of the Most High and resting in the shadow of the Almighty.

_____
_____
_____
_____

#5. Has there been a time in your life when God has shown Himself in some manner to remind you that He is large & in charge of all things?

_____
_____

#6. When God delivers His surprises, it's so important to remember to thank and honor Him for doing so. Has He surprised you lately?

My prophetic blog post is shorter this week since I'm enjoying spending time with our kiddos and grandkiddos.

May your week be filled with God pouring out His blessings from His Surprise Storehouse in heaven!

Sheila Eismann, Prophetic Seer, Blogger, & Author, publishes her weekly blog posts endeavoring to encourage others through God's word. Her writings include teaching and instructions on how to apply prophetic insights for daily living.

Please subscribe to receive new blog posts on her website at www.sheilaeismann.com. by clicking the "Subscribe" button in the far upper right-hand corner of her Home webpage.

It's Cool To Be Kind!

May 19, 2022

Inspiration

While waiting in line to vote in our state's primary election, I spotted the above wooden sign which read, "It's cool to be kind." At first glance, I thought to myself, "Well, that's cool!"

Our voting precinct is located inside an elementary school. The sign was propped up in a window near the welcome and registration area which was not only teeming with students but registered, ready voters.

<u>Snafus and Lash-ups.</u>

Technology is great when it works, correct?

Since the polls opened at 8:00 a.m., I decided to walk to the school and vote early. Not often, just early.

There were a few people ahead of me when suddenly the line came to a complete standstill.

New voting equipment had been installed and implemented for the first time. The volunteers were doing their level best to learn how to operate these "gizmo-gadgets" as my daddy used to call them.

Several steps were required which included the election worker initially typing in the information appearing on the voter's driver's license, the machine reading the license, the voter signing the screen, and on rolls the voting river.

One machine completely malfunctioned for a period of time. Those who had planned to stop by quickly and vote before heading to work were not so overjoyed by this event.

The voting wheels came to a screeching halt when a woman standing in line a short distance ahead of me attempted to select her already registered party affiliation on the machine screen.

For some strange reason, the voting system or equipment had registered her as an independent. To add further aggravation to the equation, she was informed that she could not vote right then but would have to step to the side and call a specific phone number to get this issue ironed out.

Leaning against the wall of the school hallway, the woman voter dialed the assigned number and began to explain the snafu or lash-up, whichever description you prefer. (One of my sons-in-law calls some of my descriptions "Sheilaisms." This would probably apply to the lash-up wording.)

The last line of the one-sided, loud, conversation I heard was, "What do you mean I can't vote today?"

I'm sure I'm not the only one that sensed and felt this woman voter's frustration. Would I have acted any differently? Maybe not as it's only human nature to have meltdowns from time to time. Each of us has our boiling point. Asking God, Jesus, and The Holy Spirit to lower these can be so helpful if we can think to do so ahead of time.

Please understand that I am in no way criticizing any of the events of my voter experience. I just thought it was so cool that God had already moved upon someone's heart to display the wooden sign in the archway of the window as a gentle reminder for all of us.

Kindness Can Be Cooling.

I finally made it to the desk to present my driver's license and begin the voting process. The election volunteer had forgotten her eyeglasses which necessitated that I read her the information from my driver's license, so she could enter it into the machine.

After voting, I offered a, "Thank you for helping with the voting process" to each of the volunteers with whom I came in contact in the hopes that some kindness infused into the situation could be cooling.

A gentle reminder emerges from Proverbs 15:1,

"A soft answer turns away wrath,
But a harsh word stirs up anger."

Prophetic Insights For Daily Living.

#1. Proverbs 19:22a states, "What is desired in a man is kindness."

How does kindness motivate you or other people?

#2. Has there been a time of late when someone has done something very kind for you? How did it make you feel?

_____

_____

_____

_____

#3. When an unexpected kindness comes your way, how do you respond emotionally? I was visiting with a woman who told me that when someone does something kind for her, she is completely undone. It just dissolves her into tears in a good way.

An act of kindness affects a person's heart and spirit in more ways than we can ever imagine.

_____

_____

_____

#4. In December of 2020, the Holy Spirit quickened unto me that kindness is an invaluable currency. Here's the weblink: https://sheilaeismann.com/spiritual-currency/

Kindness

After reading this blog post, would you agree that kindness is a spiritual currency?

What are some practical ways you could spend yours?

_____

_____

_____

_____

#5. God, Jesus, and The Holy Spirit infuse kindness into our lives in so many areas. Here are some that readily come to mind:

John 3:16, "For God so loved the world that He gave His only begotten Son, that whoever believes in Him should not perish but have everlasting life."

Romans 2:4 (NIV), "Or do you show contempt for the riches of his kindness, forbearance and patience, not realizing that God's kindness is intended to lead you to repentance?"

Philippians 2:8, "And being found in appearance as a man, He [Jesus] humbled Himself and became obedient to *the point of* death, even the death of the cross."

John 14:15-18, "If you love Me, keep My commandments. And I [Jesus] will pray the Father, and He will give you another Helper, that He may abide with you forever—the Spirit of truth, whom the world cannot receive, because it neither sees Him nor knows Him; but you know Him, for He dwells with you and will be in you. I will not leave you orphans; I will come to you."

1 Corinthians 13:4-8, "Love suffers long *and* is kind; love does not envy; love does not parade itself, is not puffed up; does not behave rudely, does not seek its own, is not provoked, thinks no evil; does not rejoice in iniquity, but rejoices in the truth; bears all things, believes all things, hopes all things, endures all things. Love never fails."

Ephesians 4:32, "And be kind to one another, tenderhearted, forgiving one another, even as God in Christ forgave you."

Do any of the above verses really tug at your heartstrings or speak to you?

_____
_____
_____
_____

What other Bible verses would you add to this list?

_____
_____
_____
_____

In what areas of your life has God blessed you with His kindness?

_____

_____

_____

_____

A Call to Action.

Would you please join me in a 30-day challenge to try to do at least one kind thing, large or small, for someone each day? Or if that is too long of a timeframe, how about a 10-day challenge? If you're already doing this, bravo!

Please plan to make a mental note of how this makes you feel or if you notice a difference in your life as you implement and practice kindness.

_____

_____

_____

Kindness is so necessary year-round, but especially so during an election year.

As our hot, mountain west, desert temperatures continue to rise, it's cool to be kind!

Sheila Eismann, Prophetic Seer, Blogger, & Author, publishes her weekly blog posts endeavoring to encourage others through God's word. Her writings include teaching and instructions on how to apply prophetic insights for daily living.

Please subscribe to receive new blog posts on her website at www.sheilaeismann.com. by clicking the "Subscribe" button in the far upper right-hand corner of her Home webpage.

The Way of Life Winds Upward for The Wise

May 25, 2022

Prophetic Teachings

Does studying the life of King Solomon, the wisest man who ever lived other than our Lord Jesus Christ, ever intrigue you? I've often wondered at what juncture he penned proverbs and songs and shared his God-given wisdom which flows like a river at flood stage down through the ages for the rest of us to observe. Proverbs 15:24, "The way of life winds upward for the wise," has been winding its way through my spirit for some time now.

Donna, The Gardner.

My husband and I have about five regular daily walking routes from which to choose. Like my daddy who named each of the fields on Sage Creek Farms where I was raised, I've dubbed each of the walks with a certain name. One of these is "Donna, the Gardner."

God offered up His peaceful blue sky dotted with a few, cottony, white clouds here and there on Sunday afternoon as we started our prayer walk.

Mr. Redbreast, Red Robin was bobbing along the grass searching for worms to feed his new little brood. The seven oak trees had cast their leaf coverings which resemble strands of golden, human hair. Mrs. Robin seemed to be pretty particular in selecting certain ones of these to add a little more comfort to her nest even though all of the fibers looked the same to me.

Much to our delight, as we approached the home of Donna, The Gardner, she was standing in her front yard surveying with much satisfaction the fruits of her labors.

Suddenly, I spotted what could serve as the perfect picture I'd been looking for to accompany this week's prophetic blog post! It's the lush, green vine winding its way upward sporting snappy purple blooms, which attract hummingbirds like a magnet.

Donna, The Gardner, is flat-out amazing and such an inspiration. She is Italian and speaks English sufficiently so that one can easily carry on a conversation with her. I requested permission to take the photo to which she exuberantly agreed.

Much to our surprise, Donna still mows her lawn and takes care of her beautiful yard and garden.

90 candles will soon adorn Donna's birthday cake! She told us that as she works outside, pushing her lawn mower and inspecting every square inch for weeds, she says her daily prayers. An invitation to stop by for a cup of coffee soon followed.

Later, I felt led by The Holy Spirit to consult the meaning of Donna's name, which inspired me even further as a double confirmation:

"Donna – Literal meaning: Lady

Suggested Character Quality: Dignity of Character

Suggested Lifetime Scripture Verse: Hosea 14:9,

"Who *is* wise?
Let him understand these things.
Who is prudent?
Let him know them.
For the ways of the Lord *are* right.
The righteous walk in them,
But transgressors stumble in them."

John 15, The Vine, & The Vinedresser.

Interestingly enough, our Sunday morning sermon addressed John 15, the vine, & the vinedresser.

To instruct and encourage His disciples, Jesus stated, "I am the true vine, and My Father is the vinedresser. Every branch in Me that does not bear fruit He takes away; and every *branch* that bears fruit He prunes, that it may bear more fruit. You are already clean because of the word which I have spoken to you. Abide in Me, and I in you. As the branch cannot bear fruit of itself, unless it abides in the vine, neither can you, unless you abide in Me.

"I am the vine, you *are* the branches. He who abides in Me, and I in him, bears much fruit; for without Me you can do nothing. If anyone does not abide in Me, he is cast out as a branch and is withered; and they gather them and throw *them* into the fire, and they are burned. If you abide in Me, and My words abide in you, you will ask what you desire, and it shall be done for you. By this My Father is glorified, that you bear much fruit; so you will be My disciples." (John 15:1-8.)

Many a sermon has been delivered far and wide from just these 8 verses. There's enough spiritual meat in them to preach for months, to say the least.

My one, main, takeaway from our pastor's message on Sunday was, "What vine are you plugged into?" I'll freely admit that I'd never quite looked at it through that set of vital, lifesaving, spiritual lenses.

Please notice that in John 15:1, Jesus uses one very important word which is *true*.

"I am the **true** vine, and My Father is the vinedresser." (Emphasis mine.)

In a day and age where the number of false christs is increasing, this verse echoes louder and stronger.

Jesus warns of the counterfeit ones in Matthew 24:24 and Mark 13:22, especially as we march toward the end times.

The litmus test for truth for all worldwide religions can be boiled down to one thing, and that is the deity of Christ. One can almost hear Jesus's question that He posed to His disciples when they came into the region of Caesarea Philippi, "Who do men say that I, the Son of Man, am?" (Matthew 16:13.)

It was Simon Peter who answered correctly, "You are the Christ, the Son of the living God." (Matthew 16:16.)

As we have the opportunity to witness about our Lord Jesus Christ and deliver the good news of eternal life through Him, it's paramount that we represent the real, true, life-giving Christ. (John 3:16; Romans 10:9-10.)

Gardens, Vines, & The Symbols.

The prophetic symbolism for a garden can be obvious, but I still like to consult these as The Holy Spirit may use one of them to speak to my spirit.

Gardens represent the church, spiritual growth, the heart of a believer, a place of intimacy with the trinity, eternal life, sins such as hiding in a garden, fruitfulness, and righteousness.

The Gardener is our Heavenly Father. Also, it can be an earthly one, such as Donna, The Gardner, or a spiritual caretaker.

Are you a spiritual caretaker for anyone at the moment?

_____
_____
_____
_____

Gardening itself is symbolized by the Father's business, preparation of the heart, ministry, or working in the harvest fields. (John 4:35.)

The vine speaks of Christ and His church, your life, and your relationship with Jesus, Israel, a peaceful or a poisonous vine, or reaping the harvest (vine of the earth – Revelation 14:19).

The Ways of Wisdom.

Wisdom has her own ways and was there when God created the earth. (Proverbs 8:22-31.)

Here are a couple of "wisdom reads" for you to check out:

https://sheilaeismann.com/heart-of-wisdom/

https://sheilaeismann.com/forsake-foolishness/

Prophetic Insights For Daily Living.

#1. God's way of life is the safe path that leads to eternal life. The exhortation in His word is to choose His ways to avoid the ultimate, disastrous destination of hell beneath as the last portion of Proverbs 15:24 reads, "That he may turn away from hell below."

If one studies church history, it's interesting to note that sermons preached millennia and decades ago addressed the subject of hell and the afterlife, but not so much present day. Why do you think this is the case?

In addition, there's also the element of society that doesn't believe in a heaven or a hell at all. Their view is that there's just this present earth and that's it. Fineeto!

Alas, dear brothers and sisters, gravity exists whether we believe it or not. Fire burns whether we believe it or not, and hell does as well. (Matthew 13:41-42 and 25:41.)

#2. Which vine are you plugged into?

#3. Are you being pruned at the moment? This is not a pleasant aspect of our Christian life, but it's a very necessary one. If you are, what is God pruning so you can bear even more fruit for Him and His kingdom?

#4. There's so much comfort and safety in abiding in Jesus, our Vine, and God our Vinedresser. Even though we face daily challenges, we are on the winning team every time!

_____
_____
_____
_____

#5. What are some of the practical ways that you've found and instituted to help you continue to abide?

_____
_____
_____
_____

#6. As you read over the list of prophetic symbolisms for gardens and vines, do any of these nudge your spirit?

_____
_____
_____
_____
_____

#7. Do you enjoy gardening? If so, what have you learned that you can apply to your spiritual life? We can discern so much from God's daily ways of life.

_____
_____
_____
_____
_____

A vine slowly climbs upward, similar to our spiritual life. As we walk in the Spirit, we wind our way closer to God!

Let's pray, shall we?

Father, thank You for being such a caring and loving Vinedresser. Jesus, all praise, honor, and glory go to You for helping us to abide in You so that we can continue to bear fruit. Holy Spirit, please help us to walk out every day in Your power and grace as we stay firmly plugged into the Three of You Who are The True Trinity. May our lives continue to flourish in You, and may we love all of You and our neighbor as ourselves. Teach us to number our days so that we may gain a heart of wisdom as our lives continue to wind upward in You.

We ask these things in the name that is above every name, the mighty name of our Lord and Savior, Jesus Christ. Amen!

Until the next message, SFE (Sheila, Fellow Encourager)

Sheila Eismann, Prophetic Seer, Blogger, & Author, publishes her weekly blog posts endeavoring to encourage others through God's word. Her writings include teaching and instructions on how to apply prophetic insights for daily living.

Please subscribe to receive new blog posts on her website at www.sheilaeismann.com. by clicking the "Subscribe" button in the far upper right-hand corner of her Home webpage.

The Angel, The Basket, & The Scrolls

June 7, 2022

Prophetic Visions

In Hebrews 1:14, the unidentified author reminds us concerning angels, "Are they not all ministering spirits sent forth to minister for those who will inherit salvation?" Late in the evening of May 31, 2022, an angel suddenly appeared in the Spirit. His shoulder-length blonde hair touched the shoulders of his white robe adorned with a burgundy sash tied around his waist. In his right hand, he held the handle of an antique white-colored basket filled with scrolls.

In the next scene of the vision, the angel reached into the basket and handed me one of the scrolls. As I drew it closer to my face, I was amazed to see my three initials, SFE, pressed into the red wax that had sealed the scroll.

I looked at the angel's face to see if he had a message, but he did not speak. As he smiled, I saw a supernatural reflection of a red heart in each of his eyes.

End of prophetic vision.

Angels Are Ministering Spirits.

God's angels are in service to believers in His Son, Jesus Christ. They go and do God's bidding and do not act upon their own.

The following are some Biblical examples of ministering angels:

Psalm 91:11 – Angels help to protect believers.

Daniel 6:22 – Daniel was protected in the lion's den when the angel shut the mouth of the ravenous lions.

Acts 27:23-24 – During a storm at sea, the Apostle Paul was encouraged by an angel.

Acts 12:5-7 – To help Peter escape from prison, an angel struck Peter's side and instructed him to get up quickly as the chains fell from his wrists.

2 Kings 6:15-17 – The prophet Elisha was surrounded by an army of angels to protect him from the Arameans.

Matthew 4:11 and Luke 22:43 – Following Jesus's 40 days and night temptation in the wilderness, angels tended to and encouraged Him.

Words For This Time and Season.

Carefully opening my scroll and reading it, I received scriptures relevant to:

Words of encouragement

Words of correction

Words of knowledge

Words of wisdom

Words of direction

Words of warning

There's a difference in each of our lives as to what time it is and in which season we find ourselves. I explain this more fully in a previous blog post. Here's the link: https://sheilaeismann.com/spiritual-time/

The Time of Your Life

Specific Scriptures, Signposts, & Songs.

In addition to specific Bible scriptures for my life right now, there were titles to songs. I knew that I needed to look up the lyrics to these because there would be messages in them also.

Much to my delight, I received two confirming signposts relative to the cumulative instructions on my scroll. God often goes to such unusual lengths to get His messages to us. I so love prophetic treasure hunts! I hope you do, too.

The first one appeared while I was sitting inside our car waiting for my husband to pick up an item he was having repaired. When I turned my head to the left, I just had to chuckle when I read the license plate featured in the image below.

Refocus

This license plate was fashioned in red, white, and blue which represents freedom. With so many things demanding our attention and time these days, I'll have far more freedom in Christ when I refocus upon Him, God, The Holy Spirit, and the Word of God.

While recently visiting my beloved sisters, we talked about Mary and Martha from Luke 10:38-42,

"Now it happened as they went that He entered a certain village; and a certain woman named Martha welcomed Him [Jesus] into her house. And she had a sister called Mary, who also sat at Jesus' feet and heard His word. But Martha was distracted with much serving, and she approached Him and said, 'Lord, do You not care that my sister has left me to serve alone? Therefore tell her to help me.'

"And Jesus answered and said to her, 'Martha, Martha, you are worried and troubled about many things. But one thing is needed, and Mary has chosen that good part, which will not be taken away from her.'"

On the way home, one of my sisters wanted to stop at a country café somewhere to eat breakfast. The area where we were traveling was on the industrial outskirts of a larger town which necessitated that we drive further down the road to find an eating establishment. Guess what the name of it was?

Martha's Café

A Specific Fast.

I would encourage you to read and study Isaiah 58 which describes the type of fasting that pleases God.

Written upon each of our scrolls is a specific fast to which the Lord is calling us. Not everyone can fast food and liquid for health and/or medical reasons. There are innumerable types of fasts other than these. Some will be instructed to fast certain aspects of social media, excessive personal spending, entertainment, gossip and criticism, overcommitment, unhealthy types of competition, etc.

The flesh does not like fasting at all, so be prepared for it to scream loudly!

Angels, Baskets, Sashes & Scrolls.

Delving into symbolisms for this prophetic vision, we find the following:

Angels – Ministers, guardians, God's messengers, God's presence, God's servants, spiritual warriors, worshippers, reapers, and assistants. God's angels are good ones as they did not participate in the Luciferian rebellion in heaven (Isaiah 14:12-13; Luke 10:18; 2 Peter 2:4; and Jude 1:6).

Baskets – Fruitfulness, provision, first fruits, cursed fruit, the heart, overflowing faith, or a collective group of people. The scrolls were placed inside a basket for a collective group of people who are believers in Jesus Christ of Nazareth.

Unfortunately, there's an increase in false teachings of different Jesuses, but there's only one true Jesus Who is the Son of God and the Savior of the world. (John 1:14 and 3:16-18; 1 John 4:9 and 5:20.)

Sashes – A sash is similar to a cloth belt that is used to hold a robe together when tied around the waist. Red symbolizes redemption. Perhaps the angel in the vision wearing a deep burgundy colored one speaks to the depth of Jesus's love, obedience, and sacrifice on the cross when giving His life for our eternal one.

Scrolls – Unfolding revelation (which is exactly what appeared on these individual scrolls for believers,) the Word of God, heaven, ancient book, or a personal calling or destiny. Spending time studying and completing what's written on our scrolls will help us to continue to fulfill our God-given destiny.

Prophetic Insights For Daily Living.

#1. This is not a "one scroll fits all" type of gift or delivery from heaven. None of them are the same because each of us is a unique creation of God in a different place and season in our spiritual walk with Him.

_____
_____
_____
_____

#2. When there are a lot of voices and noises, God especially wants us to press into Him, so He can reveal His marching orders to us to help us navigate continuing global challenges.

#3. Seek God and record what He shows you that is written on your scroll. We must appropriate this by faith just like we do everything else in our spiritual walk with the Lord Jesus Christ. "For we walk by faith, not by sight." (2 Corinthians 5:7).

Don't feel neglected if you are unable to see a supernatural scroll in front of you as God speaks to each of us in many different ways. Pray and ask the Lord to reveal the contents. He will be faithful to do so.

_____
_____
_____
_____

#4. Watch for prophetic signposts which will help to confirm what is written on your scroll.

If you're continuing with my suggested ongoing practice of prophetic journaling, this will really help to build your faith.

_____
_____
_____
_____

#5. Why do you deem God is sending one of His angels to earth right now with your individualized scroll versus using some other form of communication?

My prayer is that June 2022 will be a month of increased spiritual revelation for everyone. The words of our Lord and Savior, Jesus Christ, from Matthew 7:7-8 are such an encouragement, "Ask, and it will be given to you; seek, and you will find; knock, and it will be opened to you. For everyone who asks receives, and he who seeks finds, and to him who knocks it will be opened."

Until the next message,

SFE (Sheila, Fellow Encourager)

Sheila Eismann, Prophetic Seer, Blogger, & Author, publishes her blog posts endeavoring to encourage others through God's word. Her writings include teaching and instructions on how to apply prophetic insights for daily living.

Please subscribe to receive new blog posts on her website at www.sheilaeismann.com. by clicking the "Subscribe" button in the far upper right-hand corner of her Home webpage.

Grace On Our Lips

June 27, 2022

Prophetic Teachings

Glancing at the map of our country to check on current temperatures, it looked like someone had dumped an entire bottle of hot sauce on top of it! Fluid red was flowing in virtually every state. It's a cool 103 degrees in our neck of the woods today. The heat coupled with recent national developments adds a heightened challenge to speak with grace on our lips.

Solomon, the last king of unified Israel before it was split into the northern and southern kingdoms, was gifted with immeasurable Godly wisdom, influence, and earthly kingdom connections.

If you could take a wild guess, how many people do you think he spoke with during his lifetime? Perhaps that is why he included this verse when penning his sage wisdom,

"He who loves purity of heart
And has grace on his lips,
The king *will be* his friend." [Proverbs 22:11]

Before King Solomon speaks of grace on his lips much less extending his friendship, he dishes up the all-important requirement of he who loves purity of heart.

Why do you think he stated it in this manner?

_____
_____
_____
_____

The Hebrew word for grace in Proverbs 22:11 is *hen* (pronounced *khane*).

Strong's H2580 translates the meaning of *hen* as grace, favour, gracious, pleasant, precious, wellfavoured, charm, elegance, and acceptance.

https://www.blueletterbible.org/lexicon/h2580/kjv/wlc/0-1/

Sapa (pronounced saw-faw) is the Hebrew word for lips. According to Strong's H8193, the meanings for *sapa* are lip, language, speech, shore, bank, brink, brim, side, edge, border, binding, and bank (of a cup, sea, river, etc.)

https://www.blueletterbible.org/lexicon/h8193/kjv/wlc/0-1/

This paints an interesting word picture of sorts in that just as our physical lips have borders, it's as if the speech emitting therefrom should have boundaries as well.

A Polluted Heart vs. Purity of Heart

"The north wind brings forth rain,
And a backbiting tongue an angry countenance." [Proverbs 25:23]

This verse is quite a contrast to King Solomon's Proverbs 22:11 Scripture.

Grace is not on the lips of the person with a backbiting tongue and an angry countenance. The backbiting is flowing from a polluted heart, not the purity of the heart.

Thankfully, when we fully surrender our lives to God, Jesus, and The Holy Spirit, they collectively help us to purify our lives, including our speech, so that grace can be on our lips.

We are all a work in progress, so we extend grace and speak encouragement even to ourselves when needed. Perhaps this is one way in which we can practice this exhortation.

A Tree Is Known By Its Fruit.

As He delivered the Sermon on the Mount to His disciples, Jesus used the analogy of knowing a tree by its fruit.

"For a good tree does not bear bad fruit, nor does a bad tree bear good fruit. For every tree is known by its own fruit. For *men* do not gather figs from thorns, nor do they gather grapes from a bramble bush. A good man out of the good treasure of his heart brings forth good; and an evil man out of the evil treasure of his heart brings forth evil. For out of the abundance of the heart his mouth speaks." (Luke 6:43-45)

In a parallel book of the gospels when also teaching about a tree is known by its fruit, Jesus issued this warning in Matthew 12:37, "For by your words you will be justified, and by your words you will be condemned."

The fruit born from the tree is likened unto the words which end up on our lips. Grace on our lips is good fruit coming from a good tree.

"Death and life *are* in the power of the tongue,
And those who love it will eat its fruit." (Proverbs 18:21)

During the time that the Apostle Paul instructed the church at Colosse, he reminded them to put off the carnality of the old man. "But now you yourselves are to put off all these: anger, wrath, malice, blasphemy, filthy language out of your mouth." [Colossians 3:8]

Revisiting 4 Keys To Open 4 Doors.

4 Keys to Open 4 Doors

Taking some time to read and study a prophetic vision I received on September 28, 2021, might be a helpful and instructive exercise to accompany the *Grace On Our Lips* message.

Here's the weblink: https://sheilaeismann.com/spiritual-gold/

<u>Prophetic Insights For Daily Living:</u>

#1. When someone has spoken to you favorably or given you a gracious answer, how did it make you feel?

_____
_____
_____
_____

Conversely, when he or she addressed you in the opposite manner, what was your reaction or impression?

_____
_____
_____
_____

How have you felt when there was no grace on your lips?

_____
_____

#2. Are our hearts bathed in God's grace so that it flows up and out of our mouths onto our lips?

#3. How do we reflect the kingdom of God when we have grace on our lips?

#4. Here are some powerful verses to help us if we might be struggling in the area of speaking gracefully.

"So then, my beloved brethren, let every man be swift to hear, slow to speak, slow to wrath; for the wrath of man does not produce the righteousness of God." [James 1:19]

"A soft answer turns away wrath,
But a harsh word stirs up anger." [Proverbs 15:1]

"Therefore by Him [Jesus] let us continually offer the sacrifice of praise to God, that is, the fruit *our* lips, giving thanks to His name." [Hebrews 13:15]

Every time we thank and praise Jesus, we are growing fruit!

Jesus is always ready, willing, and able to help us if we will just ask Him to do so.

#5. Reading through and studying the Hebrew meanings for the words grace and lips, were there any that spoke to you or nudged your spirit? If so, I would encourage you to make a note of these.

_____
_____
_____
_____

Also, did you glean anything new or instructive from The 4 Keys To Open 4 Doors?

_____
_____
_____
_____

The last line of Proverbs 22:11 reads,

"He who loves purity of heart
And has grace on his lips,
The king *will be* his friend."

Even if you don't know an earthly king of one of the world's countries, King Jesus will always be your friend if you've accepted Him as your personal Lord and Savior (Romans 10:9-10). As we walk with and serve Him, He will help to purify our hearts and to speak graciously.

Until the next message,

SFE (Sheila, Fellow Encourager)

Sheila Eismann, Prophetic Seer, Blogger, & Author, publishes her blog posts endeavoring to encourage others through God's word. Her writings include teaching and instructions on how to apply prophetic insights for daily living.

Please subscribe to receive new blog posts on her website at www.sheilaeismann.com. by clicking the "Subscribe" button in the far upper right-hand corner of her Home webpage.

Hold The Dream!

July 4, 2022

Encouragement

Are you holding a dream in your heart and have been waiting for its fulfillment?

The three words, *Hold The Dream!*, have been ruminating in my spirit for several weeks now.

As I pressed into and relied upon the Lord for further revelation and expansion of this message, I received an expected confirmation of it by way of a telephone call.

When I answered the phone, I could sense the excitement in the person's voice as she asked me if I could recall a dream that she'd been given in 2005. This woman and her husband were working in another country at the time. What's amazing is that she recalled such vivid details of this dream down to the minutest details which are soon to be fulfilled.

Even more astounding is that one of the facilitators of the dream's fulfillment worked with this woman's husband at one point in time within our country.

God truly does have every hair on our head numbered, and there's not a sparrow that falls to the ground outside of His will [Luke 12:6-7.]

From Dream to Victory!

During our conversation, I told her that I did remember the dream which I thought was most interesting at the time given their family dynamics. I also reminded her that the fulfillment of the dream she'd been holding in her heart would be completed 17 years later.

Prophetic symbols for the number 17 are victory, complete rest, our walk with God, and the perfection of the spiritual order of things.

Suddenly, every door that needed to be opened flew wide open without any hindrance as God perfected or brought to maturity the spiritual order of things. All He was waiting for was this family to hold the dream and say *YES* to His plans and purposes.

A Dream Within A Dream.

The lady who called me and told me of her family's dream fulfillment had received her dream within a night dream in 2005.

Your dream may have also originated during the night season or it could be something that God has supernaturally deposited within your heart.

The bottom line is that God, the Supreme Dream Giver, will typically implant His dream using one method or the other.

Hold The Dream Lessons From Hannah's Life.

The Biblical account of Hannah in 1 Samuel 1-2 is a wonderful study regarding holding a dream in our hearts.

#1. History and background:

Hannah lived with her husband, Elkanah, and her tormenting sister wife, Peninnah, in the mountains of Ephraim. Suffice it to say, there were strained family relationships since Peninnah had children, but Hannah did not.

Per the Jewish custom of the day, Elkanah made his annual trek to Shiloh to sacrifice to the Lord in the presence of the appointed priests, Eli, and his sons, Hophni and Phinehas.

When Elkanah made his offerings, he would give portions to Peninnah and all her sons and daughters. Hannah received a double portion.

As the years continued to roll by, Peninnah's provocation to Hannah became more pronounced which caused her to weep and not eat. (1 Samuel 1:1-7.)

Peninnah's name means Pearl. One of the negative connotations of this prophetic symbolism is arrogance and pride. Positive ones include revelations of God's word and spiritual treasures, our faith, the gate of the heavenly Jerusalem, the Lord Jesus Christ, and His kingdom.

If we pause to think of how a pearl is formed through irritation in the shell of an oyster, we can only imagine how irritating Peninnah's conduct was toward Hannah.

#2. Hannah's Vow To The Lord:

"Then Elkanah her husband said to her, 'Hannah, why do you weep? Why do you not eat? And why is your heart grieved? *Am* I not better to you than ten sons?'"

"So Hannah arose after they had finished eating and drinking in Shiloh. Now Eli the priest was sitting on the seat by the doorpost of the tabernacle of the Lord. And she *was* in bitterness of soul, and prayed to the Lord and wept in anguish. Then she made a vow and said, 'O Lord of hosts, if You will indeed look on the affliction of Your maidservant and remember me, and not forget Your maidservant, but will give Your maidservant a male child, then I will give him to the Lord all the days of his life, and no razor shall come upon his head.'" (1 Samuel 1:8-11.)

This Biblical account continues with a challenge from Eli, the priest, accusing Hannah of being drunk while praying in the temple.

#3. In The Process of Time:

Verse 20 of 1 Samuel 1 states, "So it came to pass **in the process of time** that Hannah conceived and bore a son, and called his name Samuel, *saying*, 'Because I have asked for him from the LORD.'" (Emphasis mine.)

It's so instructive to continue to read completely through the first and second chapters of 1st Samuel as there are bountiful lessons in there full of such good spiritual meat!

Prophetic Insights For Daily Living.

#1. Are you holding a dream in your heart or spirit? God is the dream-giver. I would highly encourage you to revisit that dream and continue to pray to God and not give up on Him. If you've not written or typed it out previously, it's very important to do so to help you remember all of the details thereof.

_____
_____
_____
_____
_____
_____

#2. Our faith will be tested as we wait for our dream to be fulfilled. One can only imagine how humiliated Hannah was when she left the temple following Eli's castigating accusation. Ironically enough, God fulfilled Eli's words, "Then Eli answered and said, 'Go in peace, and the God of Israel grant your petition which you have asked of Him.'" (1 Samuel 1:17.)

_____
_____
_____
_____
_____

Here's another 17 for you as Eli's comments appear in the 17th verse of 1 Samuel Chapter 1. It's fun to look for God's little nuggets in His word.

Hannah's faith was tested to the very limit, but she remained faithful to God during her trial, lack, grief, and humiliation.

Every believer's faith will be tested to the maximum. The question is, "How will we respond and conduct ourselves until the answer(s) come?"

_____
_____
_____
_____
_____

Hannah's name means grace or favor. Will we continue to walk out our challenge in a graceful manner?

_____
_____
_____
_____
_____

For an additional faith builder, I invite you to revisit my November 11, 2020 blog post titled *The Missing Piece*.

The Missing Piece

Here's the weblink: https://sheilaeismann.com/lifes-puzzle/

#3. A dream can oftentimes be tied to our God-given destiny. We definitely see this in the Biblical account of Hannah praying for a child. Samuel was a powerful and anointed prophet, priest, and judge in Israel. God did not let one of his words fall to the ground. (1 Samuel 3:19.)

_____
_____
_____
_____

#4. What has been the specific opposition to the fulfillment of your dream?

_____
_____
_____
_____

In the **process of time** as you've been waiting for your dream fulfillment, what Christlike character or fruit of the Spirit listed in Galatians 5:22-23 has God been developing in you?

_____
_____
_____

#5. After Samuel was weaned and taken to serve in the temple of the Lord, Hannah poured out her heartfelt prayer before the Lord in 1 Samuel 2:1-10. A suggested spiritual exercise is to read carefully down through this prayer and make a note of where The Holy Spirit stops you. Record this in your prophetic journal for future reference as this may well be a comfort to you.

_____

_____

_____

_____

#6. As our dream giver, God always provides and delivers exceedingly abundantly above all that we ask or think. (Ephesians 3:20-21.) Blessings follow in the train of dream fulfillment.

Following Samuel's birth, God remembered Hannah and gave her three more sons and two daughters. (1 Samuel 2:21.)

Revisiting the telephone call I received recently, God is most assuredly going above and beyond what this family ever expected as He has added another teenager to their household. It has been a real faith builder for all of them 17 years later. I hope it is for you also as you read and study this prophetic blog post.

The words of King David from Psalm 138:3 are perfect companion ones to go along with Hannah's prayer in the temple.

"In the day when I cried out, You answered me,
And made me bold *with* strength in my soul."
As you hold the dream in your heart and wait for its fulfillment, stay bold with God's strength in your soul.

Until the next message,

SFE (Sheila, Fellow Encourager)

Sheila F. Eismann, Prophetic Seer, Blogger, & Author, publishes her blog posts endeavoring to encourage others through God's word. Her writings include teaching and instructions on how to apply prophetic insights for daily living. Please subscribe to receive new blog posts on her website at www.sheilaeismann.com. by clicking the "Subscribe" button in the far upper right-hand corner of her Home webpage.

Sheila Eismann

The Angel With The Pocket Watch

July 30, 2022

Prophetic Visions

Before the use of wristwatches which almost seems archaic now with so many people of all ages owning cell phones, men and women relied upon pocket watches. Typically, women clipped them to a blouse or uniform, and men kept them inside their front shirt or jean pocket. The angel with the pocket watch manifested in the Spirit realm during the evening of July 29, 2022.

Sitting in a mahogany-colored, antique rocking chair, this particular angel was dressed in a white robe as he looked through his thin, wire-framed round eyeglasses to the gold-colored, antique, pocket watch he held in his right hand.

When Holy Spirit zoomed closer to the watch, the time read 4:00. The numbers on this pocket watch were Arabic rather than Roman Numerals.

The prophetic vision I received showed the angel's profile from the right side, so I did not see his full face. He was concentrating heavily on the open pocket watch.

End of prophetic vision.

Pocket watches have been around since about the 1500s. We know a family member whose grandfather used his daily in the early 1900s, and when it was gifted to our relative, his grandmother told him that it had fallen out of her husband's pocket quite a bit which caused the internal mechanism to quit functioning. Thankfully, they were able to get the watch repaired to retain their precious family heirloom.

In a previous blog post that I authored on June 7, 2022, I touched briefly on the ministry of angels as outlined in the Bible with accompanying verses. There are many different types of angels who carry out the Lord's instructions as they do not act on their own. Here's the web link:

https://sheilaeismann.com/the-angel-the-basket-the-scrolls/

Personalized Scroll

Pondering The Prophetic Symbolisms.

***** While a rocking chair represents spiritual retirement, none of us in the kingdom of God is ever fully "retired" until we graduate to heaven to spend eternity with God, Jesus, Holy Spirit, and fellow believers.

When Jesus was near Jerusalem and because people in the region thought the kingdom of God would appear immediately, He delivered a teaching on The Parable of the Minas or Talents.

"So he called ten of his servants, delivered to them ten minas, and said to them, 'Do business till I come.'" (Luke 19:13.)

Irrespective of age, which is only a number, we must continually be about our Heavenly Father's business. There's no early retirement! You can read all about it: https://sheilaeismann.com/retirement/

Shekel

***** Watches or timepieces symbolize life, life's events, time itself, deadlines, departing and not wanting to be somewhere, the glory that stems from waiting on God (a gold watch), glorious calling (choosing a gold watch), or a specific time in our life (Ecclesiastes 3:1-8).

***** I was given this prophetic vision on the 29th day of July with 29 symbolizing departure. It's interesting to note that one of the meanings of watches or timepieces as referenced in the above paragraph is "departing and not wanting to be somewhere."

***** Gold (colored) pocket watch – Gold speaks of kingdom glory, the glory of God, honorable, rich or blessed (Abram was very rich in cattle, silver, and gold as stated in Genesis 13:2), refined, pure, holy, wealthy, great, powerful, anointing, first place (such as a gold medal), beautiful, valuable, or deeds done by the empowerment of Holy Spirit.

***** The number four symbolizes creation, worldwide, universal, an open door (Revelation 4:1), time (as the fourth dimension), the spirit realm (as the fourth dimension), Jesus was the fourth man in the fiery furnace with the prophet Daniel (Daniel 3:8-25), unbearable, earthly dominion, or specific dimensions such as four corners, sides, etc.

Prophetic Insights For Daily Living.

#1. As you ponder this prophetic vision, how is your spirit stirred, or what has Holy Spirit quickened unto you?

___

___

___

___

___

#2. This pocket watch showed straight up 4 o'clock. There were only the hour hands and not the minute hands. When pocket watches were first invented, they only showed the hour hand. It wasn't until around 1680 that the minute hand was added.

___

___

___

___

#3. The sense that I have is each of us is to ask God what time it is in our lives. He will be faithful to show us.

Jeremiah 29:13 comes to mind in this regard,

"And you will seek Me and find *Me,* when you search for Me with all your heart."

Also, Matthew 7:7-11,

"Ask, and it will be given to you; seek, and you will find; knock, and it will be opened to you. For everyone who asks receives, and he who seeks finds, and to him who knocks it will be opened. Or what man is there among you who, if his son asks for bread, will give him a stone? Or if he asks for a fish, will he give him a serpent? If you then, being evil, know how to give good gifts to your children, how much more will your Father who is in heaven give good things to those who ask Him!"

While visiting with a few people during the past couple of months regarding their kingdom assignments, I was informed that some of them are changing from old paradigms to new ones. This not only applies to people in full-time ministry but to fellow believers who have secular jobs and various and sundry daily responsibilities and obligations.

The changing from old paradigms to new ones would also reinforce the theme of 29 which is a departure from the old or former of whatever it was.

_____
_____
_____
_____

#4. With the antique pocket watch itself, it's possible that God could be revisiting generational ancestral family trees to bring about the creation of new or different kingdom assignments that He wants us to do now.

I would encourage you to take some time to revisit your family lineage to see how Holy Spirit speaks to you in this regard. Make sure to record what you are shown and the accompanying scriptures.

#5. Nebuchadnezzar, King of Babylon, had two powerful dreams. In the second one, he mentions there was a "watcher" coming down from heaven.

"I saw in the visions of my head *while* on my bed, and there was a watcher, a holy one, coming down from heaven. He cried aloud and said thus:

'Chop down the tree and cut off its branches,
Strip off its leaves and scatter its fruit.
Let the beasts get out from under it,
And the birds from its branches.
Nevertheless leave the stump and roots in the earth,
Bound with a band of iron and bronze,
In the tender grass of the field.
Let it be wet with the dew of heaven,
And *let* him graze with the beasts
On the grass of the earth.
Let his heart be changed from *that of* a man,
Let him be given the heart of a beast,
And let seven times pass over him.

'This decision *is* by the decree of the watchers,
And the sentence by the word of the holy ones,
In order that the living may know
That the Most High rules in the kingdom of men,
Gives it to whomever He will,
And sets over it the lowest of men.'

"This dream I, King Nebuchadnezzar, have seen. Now you, Belteshazzar [Daniel], declare its interpretation, since all the wise *men* of my kingdom are not able to make known to me the interpretation; but you *are* able, for the Spirit of the Holy God *is* in you." (Daniel 4:13-18)

In the remaining verses of Daniel Chapter 4, the prophet Daniel explains the meaning of this dream.

According to Strong's H5894, the Hebrew word for watcher refers to an angel that guards the souls of men.

https://www.blueletterbible.org/lexicon/h5894/kjv/wlc/0-1/

The angel with the pocket watch may not be a *watcher* or guardian angel; however, he certainly was intent on keeping watch on the time according to the pocket watch in his right hand. This pocket watch would have been issued to him from heaven above.

Revisiting one of the symbols for the number four since the pocket watch read four o'clock, watch for an open door in your life, those of fellow believers or someone on the world's stage.

_____
_____
_____

Until the next message,

SFE (Sheila, Fellow Encourager)

Sheila F. Eismann, Prophetic Seer, Blogger, & Author, publishes her blog posts endeavoring to encourage others through God's word. Her writings include instructions on how to apply prophetic insights for daily living.

Please subscribe to receive new blog posts on her website at www.sheilaeismann.com. by clicking the "Subscribe" button in the far upper right-hand corner of her Home webpage.

Sheila Eismann

Living In A Field Of Faith

August 17, 2022

Encouragement

The floral industry in the US is worth over $5 billion despite the fact that there was a slight decrease in numbers in the years between 2015 and 2020.

Globally, this industry is worth $18 billion. Tulips are the best-selling cut flowers in the U.S., with annual sales revenue of $65.3 million, reported by both wholesale and retail businesses.[1] While those are mega numbers to consider, more importantly, all of us must live somewhere both physically and spiritually.

On Sunday, August 14, 2022, my husband and I listened to a timely, Biblical teaching from a seasoned prophetic minister with a trusted and documented track record.

We also "soaked" in God's presence while singing along to a soundtrack recorded live in Jerusalem by a Messianic Jewish songwriter.

It has been my personal experience that certain musical notes and chords can open up and usher in the prophetic revelatory downloads and help to set the spiritual atmosphere to receive from the Lord.

Here are some examples of where prophecy is accompanied by music:

1 Samuel 10:5-6

2 Kings 3:13-19

1 Chronicles 25:1-3

Ephesians 5:19-20

As I was in the Spirit on the Lord's Day, suddenly a woman appeared in a field of assorted, pastel-colored daisies. She was probably in her late 30's or early 40's with shoulder-length, dark brown hair. Dressed in a blue, yellow, and white plaid summer dress and a large, beige sun bonnet tied with a velvet, burgundy ribbon, the woman bent down to pick one of the daisies with her right hand. Drawing it to her face, she smelled and admired it, smiling all the while.

In her left hand, she held a small Bible which was turned to Hebrews 1. This is the chapter outlining faith at the dawn of history and the ensuing Heroes Hall of Fame.

I heard in the Spirit, "Living In a Field of Faith."

Hopefully, at the time of this writing, that's where you're spiritually living.

[End of prophetic vision.]

No Boundaries & No End.

In the panoramic vision of the field of daisies, there were no boundaries and no end. It extended as far as the human eye could see.

Prophetically speaking, fields represent the church, a Christian believer, the world, or harvest.

The first part of John Chapter 4 records the powerful, spiritual encounter of the Samaritan woman and Jesus meeting at a well. Afterward, His disciples were concerned about Jesus having something to eat. His response was, "My food is to do the will of Him who sent Me, and to finish His work. Do you not say, 'There are still four months and *then* comes the harvest'? Behold, I say to you, lift up your eyes and look at the fields, for they are already white for harvest!" (John 4:34-35)

Oftentimes, Jesus used agricultural metaphors and examples in His parables, so the hearers could readily relate. He was reminding them to open their eyes and just look around as there were still so many people who needed to hear the good news of the gospel to be saved.

"How then shall they call on Him in whom they have not believed? And how shall they believe in Him of whom they have not heard? And how shall they hear without a preacher? And how shall they preach unless they are sent? As it is written:

"How beautiful are the feet of those who preach the gospel of peace, who bring glad tidings of good things!"

"But they have not all obeyed the gospel. For Isaiah says, *'Lord, who has believed our report?'* So then faith *comes* by hearing, and hearing by the word of God." (Romans 10:14-17)

Poppy, Norm, & The Morning Walk.

Our grandkiddos affectionately refer to my husband as "Poppy." A few days ago, he was quite late returning from his normal morning walk. When he arrived home, I asked him about the delay and how his walk was to which he replied with an exuberant, "Great!"

Periodically over the past decade, we would see an older gentleman named Norm walking in our area. If the occasion presented itself, we would stop and chat with him for a few minutes.

On this particular morning of Poppy's walk, at the EXACT same time that he felt a nudging from the Holy Spirit to walk across the street and speak with Norm about Jesus and salvation, Norm had received the very same leading!

Much to the pleasant surprise of both men, they had each already accepted Jesus Christ as their personal Lord and Savior, so their

names could be written in the Lamb's Book of Life. (Luke 10:20; Philippians 4:2-3, Revelation 3:5 and 21:27)

Also, this divine encounter resulted in Poppy receiving a prayer assignment regarding a member of Norm's family.

Grieved By Various Trials.

It's of the utmost importance to live in a field of faith while undergoing a trial of our faith.

Immediately following the birth of the early church as recorded in the book of Acts, the Christians were dispersed as a result of persecution which caused a dramatic growth in the number of believers and followers of Jesus Christ.

The Apostle Paul was called to minister to the Gentiles while the Apostle Peter was sent to the Jews. (Galatians 2:8)

Peter greets the elect pilgrims in 1 Peter 1:6-9,

"In this you greatly rejoice, though now for a little while, if need be, you have been grieved by various trials, that the genuineness of your faith, *being* much more precious than gold that perishes, though it is tested by fire, may be found to praise, honor, and glory at the revelation of Jesus Christ, whom having not seen you love. Though now you do not see *Him,* yet believing, you rejoice with joy inexpressible and full of glory, receiving the end of your faith—the salvation of *your* souls."

It's quite possible the reason The Apostle Peter refers to them as *pilgrims* is because they had been driven from other areas due to persecution or their ethnicity. Since they refused to participate in pagan rituals and worship man-made gods, some ended up being slaves due to low socio-economic status and lack of governmental protection.

As some of them worked in literal fields, their faith would have been tested to the maximum. They most certainly would not have been treated as royalty by the Roman Empire.

Daisies & The Number 14.

The Holy Spirit could have chosen any flower to populate the field in the prophetic vision.

According to Cathie Richardson, author of *Victorian Flora, A Language of Flowers Handbook*, "The name Daisy came from "Days-Eye" because daisies open during the day and close at night."

Daisies symbolize innocence, purity, and new beginnings.

A trial of our faith can require a new beginning as we may have to deal with loss, trauma, betrayal, persecution or any number of life's challenges.

I received this prophetic vision on August 14, 2022. The number 14 speaks of deliverance, salvation, liberty, and a double measure of spiritual perfection as one of the symbols of 7 is spiritual maturity or perfection.

This meaning goes hand-in-hand with Jesus' words listed above from John 4:34-35 regarding salvation.

"And he who wins souls *is* wise." (Proverbs 11:30b)

If you encounter someone today and feel that stirring from The Holy Spirit to share the good news of the gospel, I would urge you to do so. You may never see that person again, much less four months from now!

Life Can Be Puzzling At Times!

I've listed below a previous blog post written about the subject of faith if you'd like to revisit it for some direction and encouragement.

The Missing Piece

https://sheilaeismann.com/lifes-puzzle/

<u>Prophetic Insights For Daily Living.</u>

#1. Are you willing to share your faith in Jesus Christ with those in your neighborhood, town, and surrounding community?

_____
_____
_____
_____

#2. God has a limitless supply of faith to provide to us if we're willing and able to receive it from Him.

When our faith begins to wane, especially in the heat of battle and trials, we can bend down and pick a fresh daisy for a fresh infusion of faith. Envision a limitless field all around you!

#3. Is there someone God is laying upon your heart who is going through a challenge or trial of some sort right now? If so, how can you render practical love and encouragement to him or her?

You might even consider gifting a daisy and sharing this prophetic word along with the accompanying scriptures as there's such power in the word of God.

#4. What does *Living In A Field Of Faith* mean to you? How can you readily apply it to your life today?

#5. Pray and ask God for the Holy Spirit's gift of faith as outlined in 1 Corinthians 12:9 to help grow your faith.

#6. I would encourage you to read and study Hebrews Chapter 11. When doing so, is there a particular person with whom you can identify? If so, plan to do some further study about that person's life where it's mentioned in the Bible. For instance, Hebrews 11:22 mentions Joseph. A great deal can be learned from studying his life.

Faith is trusting in God and His love for us which is unlimited, and so should be our faith in Him. We must trust Him in all situations. Our faith is not that

He will do what we want Him to do. It is that He is God, and our faith is trusting in His wisdom and love at all times.

"So Jesus answered and said to them [His disciples], 'Have faith in God.'" (Mark 11:22)

In this prophetic vision, the pastel daisies stretched as far as you could see. Our faith in God should be as limitless!

Until the next message,

SFE (Sheila, Fellow Encourager)

Sheila F. Eismann, Prophetic Seer, Blogger, & Author, publishes her blog posts endeavoring to encourage others through God's word. Her writings include instructions on how to apply prophetic insights for daily living.

Please subscribe to receive new blog posts on her website at www.sheilaeismann.com. by clicking the "Subscribe" button in the far upper right-hand corner of her Home webpage.

[1] https://www.google.com/search?q=how+much+revenue+is+generated+by+flowers+every+year&rlz=1C1CHBF_enUS800US801&oq=how+much+revenue+is+generated+by+flowers+every+year&aqs=chrome..69i57j33i160.6213j0j7&sourceid=chrome&ie=UTF-8

My prayer is that you have been encouraged and challenged as you have worked your way through this prophetic workbook and learned so much more about The Holy Spirit and His Gifts along with the revelatory realms of heaven.

If you have never trusted Christ as your personal Lord and Savior, I sincerely hope that you would consider doing so at this very moment. To bring Him into your life, you need to admit your sin and inability to save yourself and ask Jesus Christ to save you. Ephesians 2:8-9 tells us, "For by grace you have been saved through faith, and that not of yourselves; it is the gift of God, not of works, lest anyone should boast."

Jesus has promised to save all who desire to turn from their sins and call on Him in faith. The Bible also instructs us in John 1:12: "But as many as received Him, to them He gave the right to become children of God, even to those who believe in His name:"

Taking a short walk down "The Roman Road to Salvation" is an easy way to ensure that your name is written in The Lamb's Book of Life. Instructions for accepting Jesus Christ as your personal Lord and Savior could not be made easier:

"that if you confess with your mouth the Lord Jesus and believe in your heart that God has raised Him from the dead, you will be saved. For with the heart one believes to righteousness, and with the mouth confession is made to salvation."

Romans 10:9-10

ABOUT THE AUTHOR

I'm an author, blogger, poet, and speaker who has published sixteen (16) books and contributed to three (3) collaborative works. Also, I'm third in my lineage of five female published poets and writers.

During the summer of 2020, I began writing a weekly blog post. "Prophetic Insights For Daily Living" features spiritual teachings, messages, inspiration, words of encouragement, self-reflection, application, and contemplation. My primary emphasis is to encourage others to apply the word of God to their daily lives in a very practical and meaningful way.

While I write in various genres, the west and all things genuinely western are some of my favorite things. Having worked in accountancy, agriculture, the legal field, various administrative capacities, and within the church realm, I pen fiction and non-fiction based upon varied life experiences.

Reading can take us places we've never been before as we learn and discern from the author's voice printed between the covers of a book or appearing on a digital screen. I hope that you will be encouraged, laugh, gain wisdom, and continue to read as much and often as you can.

Serving as one of the original co-founders of ICAN (Idaho Creative Authors' Network), I enjoy speaking at Women's and Writer's Conferences. One of my main endeavors is to enhance the lives of others through education and encouragement. Being a wife, mother, and grandmother, my motto is, "Teamwork makes the dream work!"

Discovery alert: Learn more about me, read & subscribe to my weekly blog posts, and discover my books at www.sheilaeismann.com.

Where to find Sheila Eismann online:

Email: sheila@sheilaeismann.com

Website: www.sheilaeismann.com

Facebook: www.facebook.com/sheila.eismann

Blog: www.sheilaeismann.com

LinkedIn: Sheila Eismann

Etsy: Sheila's and Dan's books are also featured online in Sheila's Etsy shop: www.etsy.com/shop/BooksbySheilaEismann

Sheila invites you to check out her new website **www.sheilaeismann.com** and sign up to receive her blog posts in your email inbox. Please send her an email at **sheila@sheilaeismann.com** to say hello and to let her know what ministered to you the most in this workbook or your favorite blog post. Happy reading and studying!

OTHER BOOKS AVAILABLE FROM AUTHORS SHEILA EISMANN, DAN EISMANN & DESERT SAGE PRESS which can be purchased from: www.sheilaeismann.com or www.amazon.com.

Read and study with **Sheila Eismann,** Prophetic Author, Blogger, Speaker, and Teacher, in Volume 1 of her latest series titled ***Prophetic Insights for Daily Living.*** This **231-page** workbook can be used as a stand-alone devotional, individual Bible Study, or in a group study. Sheila describes various dreams, visions, prophetic words, and teachings she's been given by The Holy Spirit from August 2020 through December 2020 which are designed to help you grow in spiritual knowledge and the operation of The Holy Spirit gifts. Each entry includes questions, contemplation, reflection, or a call to action.

Read and study with **Sheila Eismann,** Prophetic Author, Blogger, Speaker, and Teacher, in Volume 2 of her latest series titled ***Prophetic Insights for Daily Living.*** This **234-page** workbook can be used as a stand-alone devotional, individual Bible Study, or in a group study. Sheila describes various dreams, visions, prophetic words, and teachings she's been given by The Holy Spirit from January 2021 through May 2021 which are designed to help you grow in spiritual knowledge and the operation of The Holy Spirit gifts. Each entry includes questions, contemplation, reflection, or a call to action.

Read and study with **Sheila Eismann,** Prophetic Author, Blogger, Speaker, and Teacher, in Volume 3 of her latest series titled ***Prophetic Insights for Daily Living.*** This **234-page** workbook can be used as a stand-alone devotional, individual Bible Study or in a group study. Sheila describes various dreams, visions, prophetic words, and teachings she's been given by The Holy Spirit from May 2021 through October 2021 which are designed to help you grow in spiritual knowledge and the operation of The Holy Spirit gifts. Each entry includes questions, contemplation, reflection, or a call to action.

Read and study with **Sheila Eismann,** Prophetic Author, Blogger, Speaker, and Teacher, in Volume 4 of her latest series titled ***Prophetic Insights for Daily Living.*** This **235-page** workbook can be used as a stand-alone devotional, individual Bible Study or in a group study. Sheila describes various dreams, visions, prophetic words, and teachings she's been given by The Holy Spirit from October 2021 through February 2022 which are designed to help you grow in spiritual knowledge and the operation of The Holy Spirit gifts. Each entry includes questions, contemplation, reflection, or a call to action.

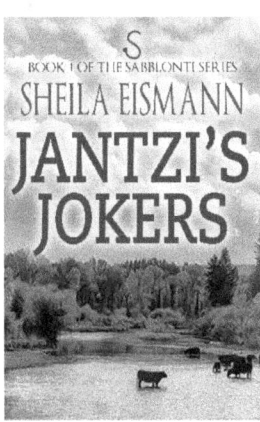

Western Fiction Book One of The Sabblonti Series, **Jantzi's Jokers**, features Jantzi Belle, the matriarch of the Sabblonti family, who has worked for decades to keep her cattle empire intact. Life takes a drastic turn when she receives a late-night visitor. The brief disappearance of her Last Will and Testament could complicate matters between her daughters, Stormy and Sarita. Stormy and her husband, Chet Castins, are struggling to work through the loss of their three children. Against all odds, drifter Wyn Moreland makes a bold move when he decides that Sarita is his beauty to rescue. The county veterinarian, Dr. Ben Shaw, is also vying for her affections. Will Wyn emerge as the winner? Just before the dawn of the New Year, revelations come forth regarding forgery, cattle rustling, and land exploitation. Will the Sabblonti Empire survive, and more importantly, who will control its reins?

The Sabblonti Saga accelerates in Book Two of the Series, **A Stormy Year**. Riding her high horse after inheriting the family fortune, Stormy Castins is determined to reinvent herself following her husband's accident. Blinded by jealousy, ambition, and naivety, she hires Less and Meg Alotto to oversee her vast high desert mountain domain. While Stormy is away, the cattle herd ends up in disarray.

Amidst the hot dry season, romance is blooming on several fronts despite a major showdown during a mid-summer celebration. The pesky Black Raven continues to wreak havoc at the most inopportune times.

Unable to overcome the vengeance which strikes by way of a mysterious range fire combined with the dire deeds of a cagey couple, the Sabblonti Ranch is in shambles just as Stormy starts to regain her senses. Humility is the prescription needed to open her eyes to realize what's truly important in life. The sparks from a belated holiday Rendevous set Chet and Stormy on their path to recovery.

Desperation explodes when heiress Stormy Sabblonti Castins calculates her dwindling fortune in Book 3 of the Sabblonti Series, **Love the Tie that Binds.** Is she capable of learning the painful lessons of having to rely upon someone and something other than inherited wealth? As her husband, Chet continues to heal from his near-fatal accident, tormenting shadows of The Black Raven lurk in the background.

These high desert hills are alive with blessed babies, enchanting engagements, skillful scavengers, sophisticated scoundrels, rich revelations, timeless treasures, and western weddings.

The Main Sabblonti Ranch house abounds with an unexpected marriage, childrens' voices, and Sir Shelton sporting his silver bell.

In a captivating story of courage, trust, and faithfulness, will Stormy still be tied in knots or find lasting love by the year's end?

Share the joys and sorrows of a mountain community in this swirling saga.

In this collection of true stories titled ***Stirrings of The Spirit***, author Sheila Eismann invites you to walk with her family through several valleys en route to some mountain tops as they learned to rely on God in the most harrowing of circumstances.

RECOGNIZE YOUR CIRCLES

A Humorous Look
Into Life's
Relationships

Have you ever wondered why you were the last one to hear of THE big social event of the year? Well, wonder no longer after reading this e-book titled **Recognize Your Circles**! When volunteering for an organization years ago, author Sheila Eismann was introduced to the concept of "the circles of your life." Since the idea was so beneficial to her, she decided to share it with all of you.

Straight from the Horse's Trough is a humorous read to assist the suburbanite or urbanite who desires to live a healthier lifestyle by growing his or her own food, but is faced with the challenge of a small space in which to do so. This e-book is chock full of how-to steps and includes pictures to remove the guesswork from the project.

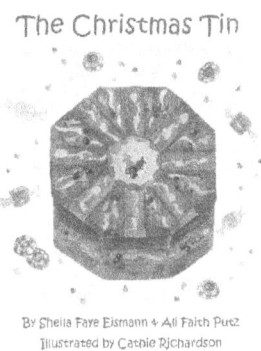

The Christmas Tin is a most delightful read for the young at heart anytime during the year. This endearing book is based upon a true story featuring the older of the two authors when she was a young girl and conveys the timeless message that "love truly is the best gift of all." Children will especially enjoy all of the colorful illustrations contained within this treasure. There's a sugar cookie recipe included in the book and a helpful holiday suggestion for the kiddos to bless someone who's not expecting it at all!

Freedom is Your Destiny! Vietnam Veteran, Dan Eismann, using combat experiences to illustrate spiritual truths, invites you to take a journey with him as he presents a rock-solid strategy for not only fighting your spiritual battles but winning the all-important war. In the midst thereof, the most vital aspect is realizing you can experience freedom and become all that God has destined you to be!

Settle into your special reading spot; grab a cup of tea or your favorite meal. Be stirred as you read and ponder **Poetry Time, Volume One**; allow Sheila's words to encourage and heal.

Everyone can use a little encouragement ~~ a dose of what is beneficial, ethical, and honorable. **Heart to Heart From God's Word** provides this for you. Penned with humor and wisdom, the daily tidbits are paired with Bible verses that convey life-changing principles which are designed for readers of all ages transcending cultures and continents. This devotional will challenge you to grow and fulfill your God-given destiny. It can also double as a prayer journal.

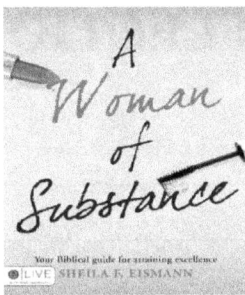

A Woman of Substance is a practical, interactive, and entertaining 12-week Bible study penned to help equip you to fulfill your God-given destiny and impact the culture for Jesus Christ at the same time. It can be used as a stand-alone study or devotional and works well in a group setting, too. It is designed for women ages junior high through adult.

ADDITIONAL NOTES & REFLECTIONS

ADDITIONAL NOTES & REFLECTIONS

ADDITIONAL NOTES & REFLECTIONS

ADDITIONAL NOTES & REFLECTIONS

Sheila Eismann

ADDITIONAL NOTES & REFLECTIONS

ADDITIONAL NOTES & REFLECTIONS

ADDITIONAL NOTES & REFLECTIONS

ADDITIONAL NOTES & REFLECTIONS

ADDITIONAL NOTES & REFLECTIONS

[i] Keesee, Ruby, Bible Studies for Women: The Gift of the Word of Knowledge (Caldwell, Idaho, 1990), PP. 1-4.

Keesee, Ruby, Bible Studies for Women: The Gift of the Word of Wisdom (Caldwell, Idaho, 1990), PP. 1-2.

[ii] Keesee, Ruby, Bible Studies for Women: The Gift of Discerning of Spirits, (Caldwell, Idaho, 1990), PP. 1-4.

[iii] Jeremiah 23:28.

[iv] AMG Dictionary – Old Testament, word 5030.

[v] Deuteronomy 18:18.

[vi] Jeremiah 20:8.

[vii] Jeremiah 20:9.

[viii] AMG Dictionary – Old Testament, word 2374.

[ix] AMG Dictionary – Old Testament, word 7200.

[x] Jeremiah 1:7, 9, 11, 12.

[xi] 1 Chronicles 29:29–30.

[xii] 2 Samuel 12:1–4.

[xiii] 2 Samuel 12:5.

[xiv] 2 Samuel 11:2–12:9.

[xv] Luke 1:5, 7, 11, 13, 16–17.

[xvi] 2 Chronicles 24:18–19.

[xvii] Acts 11:27–30.

[xviii] Acts 15:32.

[xix] Acts 13:1–3.

[xx] Jeremiah 1:9–10.

[xxi] House, Paul R. (2008) Note to Jeremiah 1:10. L. T. Dennis (Ex. Ed.), ESV Study Bible, English Standard Version. Wheaton, Ill.: Crossway Bibles.

[xxii] 1 Thessalonians 5:20–21.

[xxiii] 1 Corinthians 14:29–32.

[xxiv] Luke 2:36; Acts 2:17; 21:6.